£14.99

This book is to be returned on or before the last date stamped below.

LIBREX

D1625703

HORSES

Their Life in Pictures

Beatrice Michel
Photography by Lida Jahn-Micek

PB

PARKGATE
BOOKS

PAGE 1
The stallion is the
main contributor in
the establishment
and preservation of
social groups.
Through his
behaviour he also
influences the social
relationships within
a group.
(Andalusian
stallion in Spain.)

PAGE 2
Horses are not
loners. When they
are independent of
humans, they form
small groups.
(Andalusian stallion
in Spain.)

PREVIOUS PAGE
Horses are animals
of flight. With a fast
gallop they try to
leave any source of
danger behind
them as quickly as
possible. (Haflinger
in the Tyrol.)

First published 1990 by
PRC Publishing Ltd
Kiln House
210 New Kings Road
London SW6 4NZ

This edition published 1998 by
Parkgate Books Ltd

Translation by Dominik Kreuzer

ISBN 1 85585 015 X [1857780124]

Printed and bound in China

Horses are nosy. Sudden noise, unknown objects or strange smells attract their attention. (Andalusian stallion in Spain.)

OVERLEAF
Early summer not only means warmer days and more succulent grass, it is also the season of births, rivalry and mating. (Andalusian stallion in Spain.)

Two four-year-old
stallions from the
Camargue greet
each other.
Emulating adult
stallions, they have
already adopted an
imposing posture.

CONTENTS

THE
FAMILY

Most people think of horses as solitary animals that graze alone in small meadows. In places where horses roam free, however, they live quite differently. Whether in North America, Australia, Japan or Europe, horses left to their own devices form groups, rarely choosing to live independently of others. A group of horses is not, as may appear at first sight, just a random collection of animals. Horses live in small families, called 'harems', which are always led by a stallion. Each of these stallions has one or two, sometimes even three, mares. The mares' foals and their one- and two-year-old offspring are also part of the harem. The adult members were born to another group and joined the harem later in life

The social behaviour of the individuals within the group is determined by a set of rules. The adult animals form relationships with each other, each knowing the others, and being aware of their strengths and weaknesses. Disputes between members of a group are controlled by a social hierarchy, headed by the leading stallion. The mares recognize his leadership and obey him when he adopts his characteristic driving posture to keep them together and lead them in a particular direction. The special position of the stallion is not only

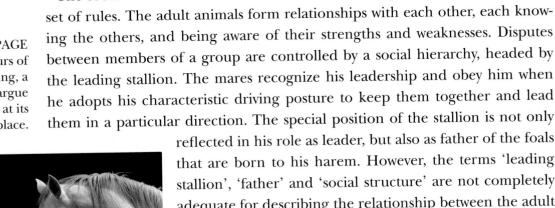

reflected in his role as leader, but also as father of the foals that are born to his harem. However, the terms 'leading stallion', 'father' and 'social structure' are not completely adequate for describing the relationship between the adult members of the harem. Animals belonging to the group do much more than simply share living space; they are friends and partners. Their affection for each other is expressed through their closeness to each other, their greetings, physical contact and grooming. Once fully established, the relationships between the various adults within a harem last throughout their lifetimes.

In natural conditions, the birth ratio of female to male animals is about 1:1; in other words, an equal number of male and female animals are born. As each adult stallion has more than one mare, this leads to an excessive number of stallions, who then organize their own, secondary groups. Groups of 'superfluous' stallions constitute this second characteristic grouping of horses. Two- to four-year-old stallions usually spend their youth in such groups, joined by the occasional young 'guest' mare. These groups could be thought of as 'waiting rooms' for future leading stallions.

There are few species in which adult animals form lifelong relationships. These include some predatory animals, such as wolves and hyenas, and apes, such as macaques and gorillas. Among hoofed animals – a group that includes horses – it is rare. In most hoofed species, such as bison, buffalo and reindeer, only the mother and her young stay together and then only as long as the young animal is dependent on her care. Once it has become self-sufficient, they go their separate ways. The males of these species seek contact with the females only during the mating season. Some establish a claim to a territory during this time – an area of their choice, defended from other males. They

A small family of horses in the Camargue, consisting of the leading stallion (right), a mare and her foal.

wait there for rutting females. In some species, such as deer or zebus, mothers and daughters stay together, forming matriarchal families. This affords the daughter a number of advantages: in her mother's presence she is less likely to be driven away by other adults and is, therefore, able to feed for longer periods of time without interruption. She also occupies a more central position in the herd and so attracts less attention from predators.

It is surprising that among the six closely related equines still alive today, only the real horses – the Mongolian wild horse and the domestic horse – as well as the prairie zebra and the mountain zebra live in harems. The Asian and African wild donkeys, the mule, the domestic donkey and the Grevy's zebras live only in mother/offspring pairs, occasionally with an older offspring also remaining with the mother. Animals of all ages and both sexes come together in larger groups for hours or even days. They also form herds which, in the case of the Grevy's zebra, can comprise several hundred animals. In temporary groups, such as herds, animals come and go as they please; they are not bound together in any long-lasting way either by rule or relationship.

Unlike these other animals, which form only occasional and temporary groups, horses have a highly-developed social structure and so must meet different demands. A stallion has to defend himself against rivals, even when he is not defending his territory. Mares, on the other hand, must learn to live together harmoniously and respect each other. Foals learn how to establish their place within a group from their experience with other members of the harem. Finally, before young animals can themselves become adult members of a harem, they must cut the ties with their immediate families, form relationships with their peers and gain the experience they will one day need to be a leading stallion or a mothering mare.

This is how horses live...

OVERLEAF
What appears at first sight to be a mere collection of Camargue horses is, in fact, several families which have all chosen the same place to sleep. At longer rests, during which the horses also lie down, the members of a family stay close together.

15

In breeding establishments, such as the Szilvasvarad stud farm in Hungary, mares and stallions are kept apart. A group consisting of only mares, such as the one in this picture, never occurs in natural conditions.

OVERLEAF
Unlike their relatives the donkey, horses like to enter the water, whether to avoid the muddy water at the edge of a drinking place or, like these Andalusian mares, to get at the nutritious reed.

EVERYDAY
LIFE

FEEDING

The history of the horse began about 60 million years ago, with its ancestor eohippus. This literally means 'dawn horse'. *Eos* is the Greek word for dawn and also the term used to describe the eocene, the era during which it lived, and *hippos* is the Greek word for horse. Eohippus had four toes on each forefoot, and three on each hind foot, with a small, nail-like hoof on the tip of each toe. In those days, this small striped animal, which was no larger than 30-40 cm (12-16 inches), lived in the huge tropical rainforests of the old and the new world, feeding on leaves, fruit and seeds. When, with the changing climate, steppes and grassland gradually replaced the rainforests, the early horses adapted to this new environment. The change from being leaf-eaters to feeding on grass, together with the development of single hooves, was probably the most impor-

A Württenberg stallion from the Marbach stud farm in Germany supplements his daily fare with leaves and small twigs. Only eventually, in the course of evolution, did the adaptation of teeth and digestive system allow the switch from eating leaves to eating grass.

tant step in the evolution of the horse. Because of its high content of coarse fibre, grass is a less easily digested source of nutrition. The teeth of a leaf-eater would not have been able to cope with it; only the evolution of the animal's molars, making them larger and coated with dental cement in the hollow areas of the enamel, enabled the consumption of harder, fibrous food without excessive wear. The large intestine increased in volume to become the dominant part of the digestive tract. There, with the help of microbes, fibrous vegetation is broken down. Because the structure of the digestive tract has adapted in this way the horse is able to live on a large variety of different foods available through the year. These include grass, foliage, fruit, which has a high sugar content, and seeds, which are rich in oil.

Ruminants, or animals that chew the cud, such as cows and oxen, can digest plants with a high fibre content, less nutritious protein and smaller amounts of sugar more efficiently than equines. A horse makes up for this drawback through selective grazing and with a higher daily intake of fodder – food passes through its digestive tract twice as fast as that of a ruminant. Looking at the wide range of ruminant species still in existence today and their large numbers compared to horses, one has to assume that, thanks to their superior utilization of food, they have spread at the horse's expense.

The food requirements of the horse have changed little since its domestication around 4000-3000 B.C. The first domestic horses still had to make do with grass which varied in quality according to the season. Later, when horses were not just ridden, but required to carry heavy loads and pull carts, fodder became a more important issue. The higher performance expected of them increased their energy requirements; their limited digestive capacity meant that grass and foliage alone were no longer sufficient. Furthermore, the time available for feeding was reduced. With the advent of crop cultivation the versatile digestive system of the horse was put to good use. The addition of barley, oats and rye to the horse's staple diet of grass, hay, straw and foliage increased its performance and, at the same time, reduced feeding times. Neither the structure and function of the digestive tract nor the feeding pattern have changed since domestication; small feeds between periods of rest correspond to the natural feeding rhythm of the horse, which has to find its own food in the wild. It feeds for periods of two to four hours and rests for an hour before feeding again. Depending on the quality of food, feeding takes up 12-16 hours of the day and is spread out evenly over day and night. On average, horses spend 60 per cent of their time feeding, 25 per cent resting and the remaining 15 per cent on other activities, such as dustbathing, walking, drinking and upkeep of social relationships. Depending on the season and the individual animal's gender and age, these percentages can deviate considerably from the norm. In winter, horses spend less time grazing and are generally less active. Yearlings, who are growing very rapidly and so require plenty of nourishment, and pregnant mares, who have to provide nourishment also for their developing foetuses, are particularly dependent on the availability of food in sufficient quantity and of quality. Despite prolonged feeding periods, lactating mares will usually lose up to 15 per cent of their normal bodyweight by the end of winter because of the poor quality of available food. Stallions can afford to be more active than mares, especially in spring. They rest just as much, but spend less time grazing. In general, young animals rest more than older ones, the very youngest spending the most time at rest. The foals are also the most active of animals and spend much of their time at play and exploring their surroundings.

During the day, horses are usually seen grazing in the morning or late in the afternoon. However, in the heat of summer, when they are plagued by insects, they often prefer to graze at night. Then, the cooling air and humidity keep

Horses in the wild spend between 12 and 16 hours a day grazing. In spring, stallions, like this Andalusian, have less time for grazing than the other members of their families because of the exhausting mating season.

OVERLEAF
Young Haflinger stallions enjoy a summer's day on an alpine pasture in the Tyrol. While grazing, they face in the same direction so as not to lose sight of anything.

Compared to bovines, horses are ten per cent more selective in their grazing. Leaves, fruit, herbs and bark from trees and shrubs enrich their daily diet. (A Lippizaner stallion from Hungary.)

the insects at bay, leaving the horses hours of uninterrupted grazing. In bad weather they face away from wind or rain. They seek refuge in preference to feeding only when weather conditions become extreme. While grazing, they walk slowly forward, making sure that they never stray too far from the group. They bite off blades of grass with their front teeth, usually just above ground level, lift their heads after several bites, chew and swallow while observing their surroundings, then lower their heads again. If grass is in short supply or covered by a thick layer of snow, they can rely on foliage, fruit and the bark of trees or shrubs, but only to a limited extent. In addition to the leaves of willow, aspen, beech and bramble, they will also eat gorse, holly, chestnuts and acorns, and sometimes they will dig for edible roots with their front hooves. They will also dig through snow to get to the vegetation underneath, choosing an area that is exposed to the wind because its covering of snow is shallower.

Camargue horses are exceptional in that a large part of their diet consists of the reed that grows in the widespread marshes of their habitat. They eat it as long as it remains green, but show a special preference for the young shoots that appear in early spring and have barely reached above the water's surface. They stand in the water for hours, nostrils partly submerged, to feed on their annual treat. Intensive grazing of the marshland results in a massive reduction of reed growth and a consequent enlargement of the free water surface. This benefits some other animals and provides an ideal resting place for migrating birds; some birds even spend the winter there. The cleared area also enables other plants, which the horses do not eat, to grow. These provide food for resting or overwintering ducks. Marshlands on which horses are kept tend to see an increased population of egrets, mallards, teals and coots. In this way, horses contribute to the enrichment and maintenance of the fauna and flora of this unique ecosystem.

Lactating mares have a particularly high nutritional requirement, as they also have to provide sustenance for their foals. (Asil Arab from the Olms-Hamasa stud farm.)

DRINKING

Horses need to consume a large amount of water. This is necessary for two reasons. First, it aids proper functioning of the bowels and of the animals' metabolism; after feeding, water containing certain secretions flows into the digestive tract. The less digestible the food, the more water is required. Second, water is essential for the control of the horse's body temperature. The amount required varies depending on how much is lost through sweating, given off via the lungs and kidneys or used to produce milk. To make up for dissipation of fluid during hot days or physical exertion, horses need to increase their intake of water. Although they prefer fresh, clear water, they often have to make do with brackish, polluted or slightly salty water. To avoid the dirt stirred up by hooves at the edge of a watering hole, they will wade towards the middle of the pond, submerging themselves as far as their bellies. Looking up regularly while they drink, they are always ready to flee from danger. Mares are more cautious than stallions. The ones that look up most often when drinking are also the ones that interrupt their grazing most readily to take flight at the slightest sign of danger. No particular animal seems to take on the role of leader on the way to or from a watering hole, although an older horse – either the leading stallion or one of the mares – usually heads the group. On arrival, it is usually the leading stallion who signals that it is safe to stay. He is also the first animal to drink.

Mothers of young foals, who require an increased intake of liquid for the production of milk, rarely stray far from a source of water. Grevy zebra stallions take advantage of this fact by establishing their territory around a watering hole. Mares, who become receptive again shortly after giving birth, will already be close by, ready to be courted and covered. Other stallions are permitted to drink, provided they are submissive to the owner of the territory. Mares are always given free access to it and young receptive females may attract the attention of the territory owner. Zebras drink at least once, often twice a day, usually in the morning and afternoon. In areas where they are hunted, they only drink at night. During the wet season they are less reliant on water, and may not seek a watering hole for two to three days in a row.

LEFT
Perhaps this English thoroughbred mare is testing the depth and temperature of this puddle with a view to rolling in it when the other mares have finished drinking.

On hot days horses not only drink more than usual, but also try to cool off by spraying themselves with water. (Hungarian half-breed mares.)

OVERLEAF
In cold weather horses move close together when resting. On such days they also avoid lying down. (Tyrolean Haflinger.)

SLEEP & REST

Adult horses usually sleep standing up and rarely lie down to rest. This probably reduces the danger of being surprised by predators. One animal of the group is always awake keeping guard. Furthermore, lying down and getting up again seems to require a great deal of effort for older animals. When an old animal has laid itself down and does not stand up, it is close to death. In one case, a very old Camargue mare who was unable to get up had to be put down. Sometimes an animal gets stuck when it does not have the strength to pull its legs out from underneath its body, for example in a small ditch. A foal, on the other hand, being much lighter and more agile than an adult horse, will usually sleep on its belly or flat on its side with its legs outstretched.

Horses avoid lying down on cold or wet ground. They fall into deep sleep only when they are lying down and wake up from such a sleep in gradual stages. During deep sleep, their sensory perception is dormant. They also appear to have some kind of dreams; they make noises – occasionally even 'snoring' – and their limbs twitch.

The members of a group are well co-ordinated in their activities. If one animal lies down or rests after grazing, it is quickly joined by other members of the family. Foals lie down beside their mothers and their older siblings take their place on her other side. Leading stallions prefer to doze next to their favourite mares. On cold nights, the animals move close together and at sunrise all activities are interrupted when the horses present their sides to the first rays of sunshine to warm their stiff limbs. On hot summer days, they seek refuge either in the shade or in areas that are exposed to the wind and free of vegetation. They spend most of the day there to avoid being attacked by insects, not so much resting as lying down repeatedly, rolling in the dust, swishing their tails and rubbing themselves against each other. Standing next to each other, facing front-to-back, they brush each other's heads with their tails to fend off the horseflies. Foals, in their desperation to escape these irritating pests, even put their heads between the rear legs of their mothers.

In the Camargue, a haven for insects, all the harems spend the hot midsummer days together. Leading stallions even tolerate the close proximity of rivals during this time. This closeness is to everyone's advantage, as the insect stings are spread out over a larger number of animals. As well as sucking a surprising amount of blood, the horseflies, which are about 2 cm (3/4 inch) in length, are transmitters of numerous diseases. Solitary animals are stung more often than animals in a group and darker animals also attract more insects.

This Haflinger foal from Vorarlberg in Austria rests its chin on the grass while he sleeps. Foals lie down more often than adults.

32

GROOMING

Physical comfort is an important part of a horse's daily life. The mouth, teeth and front edges of the hind hooves are all used for cleaning and grooming the horse's coat.

Despite their relatively rigid backs and limited ability to stretch their legs sideways, horses are surprisingly agile when they need to scratch their heads or behind their ears. Balancing on three legs, their heads lowered to the ground, they are able to reach these areas with ease. All horses like to roll in sand, on dry, vegetation-free patches of ground or in snow. Before rolling, the animal walks around the patch several times, head lowered to smell the ground and scratching it to test its suitability. Then it lies down to rub one side of its body, swings out with head and neck and, with jerky, bending and stretching movements, rolls on to its other side. This activity invariably has a 'contagious' effect on other horses, which will soon join in. Mares in the later months of their pregnancy and old animals find it difficult to roll over and usually get up after rubbing one side to lie down again on the other. Some animals love to roll in mud, which may sometimes lead to comical situations. A Camargue stallion, whose coat was caked with a dark layer of dirt after a mudbath, ran towards his mares. On seeing him, they panicked and took flight. Puzzled, the stallion looked at his mares, who, with quickened breathing and cocked ears, were cautiously observing him from a distance. Only when he whinnied did his mares realize who they were actually looking at. Very young foals, who have never witnessed a dustbath, sometimes run away from their mothers when they see them rolling in dust. When they have rolled or are thoroughly soaked,

This Lippizaner foal is already struggling more than his contemporaries to scratch his back. Such places are best reached in pairs during mutual grooming.

LEFT
A Lippizaner stallion from the famous Austrian Piber stud farm tries to scratch his chest using his incisors.

OVERLEAF
Rolling on the ground helps to get rid of the thick winter coat in spring and enables this Shagya-Arab mare to defend herself against insects in summer. The foal has to evade the kicking legs of its mother.

horses shake regularly. This shaking movement begins at the head and then continues along the length of the whole body to the dock or fleshy part of the tail – a strange experience for a rider!

Most horses like to wade in water. They hit the water with their front legs, spraying themselves all over, but roll only in shallow puddles, if at all. Horses are good, powerful swimmers with a lot of stamina. Their relatives, the donkeys, on the other hand, exhibit a severe dislike of water. Even the smallest water-filled ditch presents them with a serious hurdle, which they will far sooner walk around than paddle through.

Horses nibble themselves with their incisors wherever they can reach – chest, fore and hind legs, belly and dock. They require the assistance of a friend,

however, for the areas that they cannot reach. Using a distinctive facial expression, a horse will invite a friend to a social grooming session. If the other horse accepts the invitation, they scratch the tops of each other's heads and their withers, before working their way across the whole back and rump to the dock. This form of grooming is particularly common in spring, when horses need to rid themselves of the loose, itching hair of their winter coats. They often nibble each other for up to ten minutes without interruption. This behaviour also serves to strengthen their bonds of friendship. Mares and their foals usually groom each other. So, too, do brothers and sisters, young animals of the same age and leading stallions and their favourite mares. It appears that grooming also has a soothing effect on young animals.

During the moulting season and when plagued by insects, such as flies and ticks, a horse will rub itself against any firm surface it can find, including another horse. Insects that settle on a horse's ears, eyes and chin are removed by the horse rubbing its head against its own extremities. Using the dock frequently for this purpose usually results in worms. Standing next to each other, horses rub their foreheads against each other's shoulders and chests, and their lower jaws and throats against each other's backs. Often a passing animal will push itself under the neck of a bystander to brush insects from its neck and back – a method which is very popular with donkeys. It is also used by donkey stallions to block the path of a subservient male and prevent his approaching a rutting female. To fend off insects from back or belly, they throw back their heads, mouths closed, or quickly pull one rear leg up against the belly. Actively twitching individual muscles in the skin, swishing the tail and heavy stamping are also used to fend off pestering insects. Other horses, any inanimate object and the wind are the only defences a horse has against insects. Even insectiverous

A Camargue
stallion enjoys a
sandbath. These
areas in the
meadow gradually
increase in size
with daily use.

birds merely use the back of a horse as a convenient resting place, perhaps warming their feet on it in winter. The birds search for their food – insects that have been disturbed by the horses – on the ground and will even walk between the legs of the grazing animals. These sorts of birds have become a regular sight in the Camargue only over the past 30 years. More recently, other birds that are not insectiverous, have been observed imitating their behaviour. They also perch on the backs of the horses, but unlike their role models, they actually pluck loose hairs from the horses, which they then use to line their nests. The horses endure this plucking with stoicism and they may even welcome it. Only young foals dislike it and try to rid themselves of their passengers.

OVERLEAF
Demonstrations of
rank between
stallions always
begin with postures
to impress, which
show the strength
and elegance of this
Asil-Arab from the
Olms-Hamasa stud
farm. A similar
posture, albeit less
distinctive, is used
when courting a
mare.

RIVALS
AND HIERARCHY

Andalusian stallions demonstrate their strength to each other on a Spanish beach.

The stallion of a harem and his mares are grazing peacefully in a valley. Suddenly, another stallion appears on the horizon. The first stallion looks up and observes the intruder. They walk slowly towards each other, stop at a respectful distance and stare at each other again. One of the two paws at the ground, smells an old dung heap, excretes over it and then watches the other copy this behaviour. Both return to their mares, who have, in the meantime, peacefully continued grazing – end of confrontation.

If one of the two is not deterred by the imposing posture of the other, he challenges him. With the powerful thrust of his hind legs, the reaching out of his foreleg and the slightly bent neck, chin proudly held against his chest, this stallion is reminiscent of a dressage horse in extended trot. How many riders know that this elegant movement is derived from the intimidation tactics of a free stallion who has seen a rival and is heading towards him in this posture? The ensuing confrontation is no less impressive than the imposing trot, but not as dangerous as may be thought. As if in slow-motion, their necks bent, the two stallions face each other, approaching until their nostrils meet. Moving slowly forward, they touch and smell each other's flanks and dock area. Now and again, with a kind of squeak, they jerk up their heads and stamp the ground with a foreleg. A ritualized show of strength, a demonstration of rank is in full swing. The confrontation usually ends rather less impressively than the way in which it started. One of the horses smells and paws at a dung heap, makes a few steps forward and excretes over it. Depending on the reaction of the other horse, it now becomes apparent which of the two is the higher ranking. If, after both horses have smelled the heap, one of them excretes over it again, he is the dominant animal and the subservient stallion trots off. The important symbolic nature of this action manifests itself in the fact that, when there is no dung in sight, the horses excrete on a heap of soil or rabbit droppings. Sometimes, presumably because their bowels are empty, they do not excrete at all and simply mime the action of doing so.

When a stallion has proved his status in combat and has conquered mares, he then has to be able to keep them. Frequently herding the mares helps to keep them together. Through his exclusive claim to the mares, however, every other stallion becomes his rival and he has to prove himself against them. If food, water and mares are abundant, stallions and their harems share their living space. Since they are liable to meet frequently, they have to find a way of living together despite their rivalry. To fight at every encounter would be too dangerous and the risk of injury far too great. By developing a means of demonstrating their rank, they appear to have found a way of defusing their encounters and controlling their co-existence. This enables stallions that know each other well to forego the customary greeting

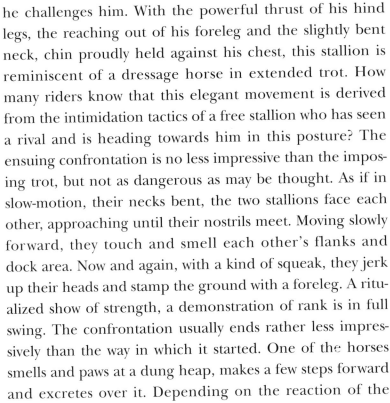

TOP
Before determining their relative ranks, these horses try to intimidate each other with a 'canter of pride'.

BOTTOM
Their excitement rises as these horses sniff each other's flanks. They squeal and each lifts up a front leg and scratches the ground.

Rearing, pushing, tossing their heads and chasing – the game has started. Playing at fighting – horseplay – is the most popular pastime among young stallions and serves as a practice for the real situation. It also helps to determine the strengths and weaknesses of contemporaries.

ceremony; excreting or not excreting, is sufficient to indicate their relative ranks. It is no longer necessary to determine which is the stronger of the two. The stallion which is higher in the social hierarchy merely adopts an imposing posture and excretes occasionally to confirm his position as head of the family. Ownership of mares is the true status symbol of a stallion.

Sometimes, however, two stallions share a harem. Their relationship with each other is also subject to a hierarchy, which determines which one of the two may copulate with the mares. Thus, the hierarchy among stallions not only controls the co-existence of different groups, but also operates within a group.

Biting during a 'playfight' looks more dangerous than it actually is.

The purpose of these rules also becomes apparent in connection with other matters. For example, when water is in short supply and a number of harems have to share a watering hole, status within the hierarchy determines the order of access. Larger groups are dominant over smaller ones and can chase them from the watering hole or stream. As two stallions together jointly own more mares than a single stallion, these groups are at an advantage. If a large group approaches a watering hole, smaller groups often retreat voluntarily. If demand is great, smaller harems may have to

wait for a long time – often as much as five hours – before gaining access to the source of water. The distance of the harems from the watering hole, as well as the order of the harems while they are waiting, reflects their positions in the hierarchy. Single mares or stallions have to give way to all harems before being allowed to drink. Confrontations can occur when two closely ranked stallions want to drink at the same time. They threaten each other, rear and try to drive each other away. The mares actively support their stallions in such confrontations, biting and threatening to kick the mares of the other harem.

OVERLEAF
A Camargue stallion whose mating has been interrupted tries to gain some respect by stamping his front leg.

Not every encounter between stallions leads to a dung ritual. Sometimes an inferior animal avoids conflict through evasion. Even the rules of excreting are not always strictly adhered to. The leader of a harem sometimes forgoes excretion on meeting a young stallion and may even permit an inferior stallion to excrete over his dung. However, if a young stallion does not accept defeat when a leading stallion covers his heap, a fight ensues. This situation arises when a bachelor wants to take one of the stallion's mares. His success does not depend on size or strength alone; other skills, such as the speedy evasion of hoof-hits and the ability to reach his opponent's vulnerable head, throat and legs with his teeth or hooves, are just as important.

The tussles and playful fights between young stallions probably serve to practise these skills and may also establish a provisional ranking, which will partly determine their future social lives as leading stallions. Being at the top of the hierarchy is not only advantageous where access to water and feeding grounds and defence of sheltered locations are concerned. Leading stallions have at least two mares and are able to defend themselves against much younger rivals. In effect, this means that they are the most successful in terms of reproduction, fathering more foals than any other stallion. In general, the sons of higher-ranking mares seem to stand a better chance of attaining this status than those of lower-ranking mares.

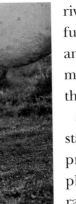

Two established leading stallions are sniffing a dung heap. It is not yet known whether the excrement of a horse carries its individual scent, like the urine of dogs.

Social hierarchy is not only important in the life of a stallion, but also plays a role among mares. Their position primarily decides priority at the drinking and feeding places. No complex rituals are required to assert their rank; laying back the ears is sufficient to put a subservient mare in her place. If she does not make way, she risks a painful bite or kick from the hind hooves of the challenging mare. Within a family of horses, the oldest mare is almost always the highest-ranking one, retaining this position for many years. Her offspring also benefit indirectly from her position. A mare with a suckling foal requires about twice as much protein as a mare without a suckling foal. When food or water are in short supply, the mare's rank can decide the survival or death of her foal. Only the mother's good physical health guarantees a supply of milk of sufficient quality and quantity. Furthermore, higher-ranking mares allow their foals to suckle longer than the usual seven to eight months before weaning. Sons of high-ranking females appear to gain the better prerequisites for a high position during their time in a bachelor group.

This inherited advantage does not apply to daughters, however. A young mare takes the lowest-ranking position at the start of her years of motherhood, regardless of her mother's rank. It also makes no difference to her position in the social hierarchy whether she chose to leave her family to join another group or was chosen by a stallion.

A playful fight between an older stallion and a younger one, whose coat is not yet completely white. By rearing, both try, in turn, to avoid the attempts of the other to bite their throats, while at the same time getting into a better position.

51

If two Camargue stallions run into each other without warning, they do not have time for a careful approach in a posture designed to be imposing. Rearing and herding together their respective harems defuses the situation.

ESTABLISHMENT OF THE FAMILY

B ecause of his dominant position, the leading stallion decides which individuals are allowed to live in his harem. Besides the herding of his mares, his characteristic behaviour includes sexual activity, friendly contact and grooming. His attention in these activities is directed mainly towards the mares, which ensures the long-term survival of the harem. Lack of offspring does not change his devotion. For example, one particular Camargue stallion stayed with his mare for years, even though an abortion had rendered her sterile. When a stallion is not defending a territory, he just keeps rivals away from close proximity of his mares. A demonstration of his strength and his imposing behaviour show other stallions that the mares are his. However, the stallion is also the motivator in the foundation of a new group. Every adolescent stallion has the desire to become a leading stallion. At times a hefty battle of rivalry is fought for the possession of mares.

Established leading stallions do not take every available opportunity to acquire a new mare. If, for example, a lost mare stumbles upon a harem, the leading stallion of the group chases her away. For bachelors or former leading stallions, who are always on the look-out for mares, it is different. They have a number of ways of acquiring mares. Their success depends on the method they employ. Deposing a leading stallion, and hence taking over a complete group, is certainly the most dangerous. First of all, the leading stallion has to be very old and weak, injured or ill. To drive a leading stallion from his harem requires considerable courage, skill and strength, which bachelors have not yet acquired and former leading stallions no longer have. In addition, successfully deposing a leading stallion can cause other problems for the new owner of the group; the conquered mares join forces against him. Although, in normal circumstances, mares show aggression only towards other mares or young animals, they will reject this newcomer. They will kick him and refuse to accept him as their leading stallion. Only the lowest-ranking mares quickly adjust to the new situation. The stallion has no choice but to put up with the rebellious mares. To gain the upper hand, he herds them continually, biting them if necessary, in the hope that this will break their resistance. His future as leading stallion depends on his ability to establish himself as head of the whole group. The smaller the harem, the greater are his chances of success. If his new harem contains several mares, some of whom fail to accept him, he can usually keep just one or two, leaving the others to another stallion.

Another tactic involves 'creeping in'. A bachelor chooses a harem that is led by a weak or injured stallion and approaches the mares. When he is attacked by the leading stallion, instead of confronting him, he takes flight, only to return to the mares minutes later. This situation can last months, until the vigour with which the older animal defends his mares noticeably diminishes. As a result of his constant proximity, the mares gradually get used to the young stallion. Whether he chooses to chase the leading stallion away or just to take

PREVIOUS PAGE
Having given birth, this Camargue mare is desirable to young stallions. Her leading stallion, who is greeting her with his imposing posture, will not move from her side during this time.

A Camargue stallion signals to his newly attained mare that she is no longer able to return to her old harem.

Whether a stallion is able to keep a newly conquered mare and defend her against rivals depends on the level of his experience.

one or two of his mares, he stands a very good chance of becoming their new leader because of their gradual acceptance of him.

Females on heat present the most direct and promising opportunity for obtaining mares. The chosen mare must still be young, however. An older mare on heat, who, through year-long membership of a harem, has become an inseparable part of that group, will vehemently resist any young, inexperienced stallion's attempts to steal her away. On the other hand, young mares who leave their families during their oestrus are easy prey. The behaviour of young zebra mares on heat is said to be so distinctive that they are recognizable as being receptive from a long distance. They attract the attention of all bachelors in their vicinity. However, bachelors can also be very choosy.

Their attention is directed towards young mothers, who have just given birth for the first time. They seem to prefer mares which have already proved their reproductive ability. The risk of encountering a determined defensive stallion during an attempt to steal such a mare is greater than the risk he would take if he were to try for a 'teenager' on heat, but not as great as if he tried to steal an older, well-established mare. Younger mothers in a harem are not protected by the stallion to the same extent as the older mares and not at all if he is their father. A good opportunity for a bachelor is when a young mare, whose foal is still struggling to keep up, falls some distance behind the group. On discovering her, he rushes towards her and tries to drive her even further away from her group. This usually attracts other bachelors, who also approach. The young mother defends herself with teeth and hooves against these unknown animals who are trying to keep her away from her group. At the same time she has to protect her foal from being bitten or kicked in the fight which now breaks out among the stallions. If the mare escapes her ardent suitors, the young stallions usually have to give up. The mare and her foal flee back to her group. The young stallions, meanwhile, decide, on neutral ground, who is to

become her new owner. They engage in all available means of combat. Age, experience and also courage and determination decide the outcome of the fights. An older bachelor who plans to form his own family usually fights with more determination than an older stallion who merely wishes to add a mare to his harem. If a contestant succeeds in manoeuvering himself between his rival and the mare, he has a good chance of success. After a tiring combat, the defeated animal finally retreats. The victor has passed the first test on his way to becoming a leading stallion. Now he has time to deal with his new mare. If she attempts to return to her harem, he signals to her, with lowered head and laid back ears, that the way back is blocked. He does not move from her side and repeatedly tries to get close to her. The young mother, on the other hand, still tries to kick him. Patiently, he evades her attacks and increases his effort to make contact with her by means of friendly gestures. Her resistance fades very gradually and only after many days does it cease completely.

A pair of young stallions that have grown up in the same group of bachelors often form a close friendship. Such pairs also approach older mares that have just given birth. Two intruders are difficult opposition for a leading stallion; if he fights one, the other tries to separate his mare from the group. If he charges at that intruder, the other tries to steal the mare. Usually he has no choice but to give up the mare and round up his remaining mares to bring them into safety. From now on, this mare will have two leading stallions of which only one is actually in charge. Only the dominant of the two courts her when she is on heat, while the other attempts to keep other stallions away. It must be assumed that the subservient of the two stallions gains from this coalition by being able occasionally to copulate with the mare – an opportunity which would otherwise be denied this weaker and, therefore, presumably unsuccessful animal. This subservient position may also have long-term advantages; the lower-ranking stallion will later have the opportunity to leave with one of the mares or may take over the whole harem if his partner becomes ill or is injured. As the mares will already have accepted him, he will not have to assert himself against them in the way a newcomer would.

To a considerable extent, the balance of a newly-formed group depends on the experience of the new owner. Young stallions who have formed a family for the first time often lose their mares. If a young leading stallion loses in combat, he returns to live with his peer group of bachelors. Then, one day, strengthened and more experienced, he ventures out into the field again – this time, perhaps, with greater success.

SEXUAL BEHAVIOUR

COURTSHIP & MATING

There are two phases in the oestrous cycle of a mare: the oestrus or heat and the dioestrus or the period between two cycles. Receptiveness lasts, on average, about five to eight days; from the end of a mare's heat to the next oestrus is 18 to 27 days. After giving birth mares quickly become receptive again – as a rule within seven to 11 days. Poor physical condition can delay the oestrus by up to 20 days. Mares are not receptive all year round, only at particular times. Their first cycle usually begins early in April when the days get longer. Among other things, the amount of light received by the eye triggers the start of the cycle. It affects the pituitary gland at the base of the brain, which regulates the release of sexual hormones. If, for some reason, the mare is not covered by the end of August, she does not become receptive again until the following spring. This limited period of receptiveness prevents pregnancy later in the year. A late birthday would reduce the foal's chances of survival; foals are born 11 months after conception.

After only a few weeks, colts begin to take interest in the excrement of their mothers. Having smelled it, they pass their own urine over it.

The first signs of heat shown by one of his mares attracts increased attention from the stallion. If the mare begins regularly to spread her hind legs and lift her tail, holding it to one side, she will soon be receptive. For the time being, the stallion restrains himself, only trying to approach the mare to sniff her rump, while nickering quietly. He is cautious because he might still be rebuffed by the mare. If he crowds her and tries, for example, to put his head on her croup, he risks being kicked. He is particularly interested in her urine, which she passes more frequently during this period. He tests each of her urinations, after which he fleers or makes a characteristic grimace. On the second or third day of her heat, the stallion becomes more active. He greets the mare more frequently with a posture designed to impress and with a typical noise which lies somewhere between nickering, squealing and puffing. Now, when he smells her genitals, she responds by lifting her tail and pushing her rump against his chest. He touches her flanks and neck with his nose and nibbles her legs and belly. This enables him to determine her readiness. If she is not ready, she will buck, squeal and run off. If, however, she turns her head towards him, touches his nose and allows his courting behaviour, he puts his head on her croup and mounts her. This courtship and the ensuing copulation occur several times a day when the mare is at her most receptive, usually after a prolonged period of rest. Young mares often appear to be somewhat coy and tend to make the stallion wait longer than older mares.

As the stallion is in the constant company of his mares, he is able to judge exactly when they are on heat. As ovulation takes place near the end of the oestrus and because the stallion's sperm is fertile for only two days, degenerating rapidly inside the mare's vagina, she needs to be mounted frequently to ensure conception. Thanks to the stallion's obliging nature, the mare is almost certain to be fertilized. Horses in the wild have a success rate of 95 to 98 per cent; in other words, only two to five mares out of 100 do not become pregnant. The rate of conception on a stud farm is much lower. For the English thoroughbred, for example, it is 40 to 70 per cent. One reasons for this lower rate is that, as mares and stallions are kept separately, the breeders have to observe and correctly interpret the mares' signs of heat. However, this does not necessarily correspond with the ideal time of reception. It is also possible that the forced and artificial nature of the situation has an effect on the chances of conception. Certainly the horses' sexual behaviour in this situation is severely limited. The two partners are led towards each other by hand and hardly have time to get to know each other. The time allowed for courting is reduced, being inhibited by manipulation – for example by putting a muzzle on the mare or tying her limbs. The rituals of courtship may even be completely done away with by the management of the stud farm.

In the wild, mares usually show no particular interest when their stallion copulates with another mare. However, jealousy between two mares has been observed. The mares were receptive at the same time, the higher-ranking one pushing and kicking the stallion when he was was mating with the other mare.

If the mare has a young foal, it stands beside her while she is being courted and mounted. The unaccustomed closeness of the stallion seems to unsettle him, however, and he frequently adopts a subservient expression. Yearlings, on the other hand, try to keep courting stallions from their mothers by repeatedly pushing themselves between the couple and bucking against the stallion. Particularly adamant youngsters have to be put in their place by a bite from the stallion. After all, their own mother is of no sexual interest to them.

Stallions take their time when they are courting a mare. By sniffing this Lippizaner mare from the Szilvasvarad stud farm, the stallion is able to ascertain whether she is ready for mating.

OVERLEAF
For the time being, this stallion keeps his distance from the mare. Her attentive face and forward-pointing ears declare her readiness for coupling.

63

Instead, they try their luck with others. Even if the stallion of the harem does not intervene, they are unsuccessful because the mares themselves will fend them off. Sometimes more mature youngsters, who have not yet joined a group of bachelors, still play at protecting an older mare on heat. If the leading stallion wants to copulate with her, he meets more resistance than he would with a yearling. The young animal lays back his ears and presents his hindquarters to the leading stallion, ready to kick, while simultaneously adopting his subservient expression – a sign that he still accepts the older and superior stallion as higher ranking. Sometimes, the leading stallion will allow the young animal to copulate with one of his mares, although the chances of conception are very small. The ability of stallions of this age successfully to cover a mare is highly questionable – at least in the case of wild Mustangs. Their sexual organs are not fully developed until they are three years old, by which time they will, of course, have left their families.

The stallion is able to test whether the mare is in oestrus by means of certain substances in her urine. It is no surprise, therefore, that the stallion shows an interest every time the mare urinates. The stallion also tests the urine of his mares outside the reproductive period. He smells both their urine and dung, frequently fleering afterwards, and passes water over them. This behaviour is seldom displayed by mares. It is interesting to note that the behaviour of a stallion towards urine and dung changes as he grows up. Adult stallions, for example, pass water more often than young ones, more frequently covering the waste of others. The ability to control the amount passed, and hence the ability to urinate more frequently, seems to be developed only in adult animals. Leading stallions do not cover just any waste with their urine, but almost exclusively that of their own mares, although they do test the excretions of other mares. This leads to the assumption that they can

distinguish the waste of other mares from that of their own. How often and, more specifically, whose waste is covered depends not only on the age of the animals, but also on their social position. A young stallion, up to the age of two, who still lives with his family, covers both his mother's waste and that of the other mares of the harem. If he is taken into a new harem, he ceases to take an interest in the waste of the mares of his former harem, including that of his mother, concentrating, instead, on that of the new mares. This behaviour enables both old and, probably,

young stallions to express their relationship with certain mares. Young stallions do not appear to be scared off by the presence of another stallion's urine on the dung or urine of a mare, even though this suggests that the mare is already accompanied by a dominant stallion. The common interest of old and young stallions in the same waste often causes them immediately to approach the place at which a mare has passed her waste and urinate over it. Disputes about superiority and demonstrations of ownership are not at issue. A young stallion is not prevented from covering waste by either his father or another stallion of

In natural herds, the act of copulation is repeated many times in the three to five days during which the mare is in season.

the group. After both animals have sniffed the waste, the older horse not only permits the younger to urinate, but sometimes even gives him priority. Young stallions are equally tolerant of each other, queuing up to pass water over a dung heap. Young, 'homeless' stallions that have left their families in search of a new group show no interest at all in the waste of mares. Older bachelors, on the other hand, that live in groups of their own without mares, often search for mares' dung heaps or urine, sniffing the ground like dogs. They smell each area carefully and fleer – this tells them a great deal. As stallions are in the habit of depositing their waste over dung heaps near watering holes and along-side paths, choosing the same places each time, large and conspicuous dung heaps eventually accumulate in these places. When young or leading stallions encounter such places, they can determine whether other animals frequent the area and how long ago they passed by. Places at which a harem has rested are also revealing; as animals usually pass their waste after a prolonged rest, mares on heat may be discovered.

PREGNANCY

Towards the end of a mare's period of heat, ovulation takes place. Pregnancy begins with conception – the fertilization of the ovum by a sperm – and lasts for about 336 days, that is, 11 months to within a few days. The duration varies slightly, depending on the age and breed of the mare and the time of conception. Older mares do not carry so long as young ones, thoroughbreds somewhat longer than cross-bred animals, and colts are usually carried a few days longer than fillies. Mares covered early in the year often carry longer than ones that mated later. It seems likely that good nutrition during the middle months of pregnancy can reduce its duration. Whether pregnant mares go full term depends on a variety of factors. For one thing, the age of the mare is decisive. Up to the fifth year of their lives, mares give birth to fewer foals than in the following years. In a healthy environment, two-thirds of young mares give birth; in less than perfect conditions only about half do. This is probably related to nutrition. It is known that a lack of protein in the third to fifth week of pregnancy can lead to a miscarriage. It is also easier for a pregnant mare to complete her pregnancy within a stable family. A forced change resulting from theft by another stallion deprives a mare of much of her strength. In addition, integration into the new harem involves coping with the aggression from the other mares. Finally, as newcomers always take the lowest place in the hierarchy, they also have to make do with food of lower quality.

According to Arabic horse-breeders, the pregnant body of a mare is a treasure chest full of gold.

During the first six months, the foetus develops relatively slowly. After 150 days, for example, it measures a mere 20 cm ($7^3/_4$ inches). At that stage, all the organs are present, albeit not fully developed, and the foetus weighs 3-6 kg ($6^1/_2$-13 lb). In the following months, it grows quickly, gains weight rapidly and its coat begins to develop. At birth, the foal will weigh 30-60 kg (66-132 lb) and measure 75-145 cm (30-57 inches) from head to dock.

The birth of twins is very rare among horses. There appears not to be enough room in a mare's uterus for the simultaneous development of two animals. At a certain stage of pregnancy, the competition between the two foetuses becomes so great that one of them dies, causing an abortion. If they are carried to birth, they are either stillborn or too weak to survive longer than the first hours of their lives.

At birth, a foal's living conditions change dramatically. For 11 months, he has been fed, cushioned and kept warm and safe. At birth, as at no other time in his life, is the demand to adapt to a new situation as great. He has to breathe, stand up while coping with gravity, maintain his body temperature within a certain range and excrete his waste products. Surprisingly quickly, he will master these skills without any problems and, with the help of his mother, eventually grow up to be a fully fledged member of his family.

OVERLEAF
A mare in the Camargue gives birth among the familiar members of her harem, who pay little attention to the event.

THE
BIRTH

In regions were there is extreme seasonal variation in weather conditions, the quality and quantity of food available varies considerably. It is, therefore, advantageous for a foal to be born at a time which offers the best chance of survival. In the northern hemisphere, most foals are born in spring, between April and June. The birth usually takes place at dawn, which is convenient in that it leaves the mother and her newborn all day to get to know each other and allows time for the foal to learn to stand up and follow its mother before the night sets in. To a limited extent, a mare can regulate the time of birth. Domestic horses tend to wait for darkness to give birth, when they will not be disturbed by stablehands and other people. In natural conditions, the mare remains with her family to give birth. She is surrounded by familiar animals, who pay hardly any attention to the process.

Various signs precede the birth. The udder swells in preparation for the production of milk. Sometimes small droplets of milk form on the teats. A swelling of the pudenda indicates multiple loosening of the pelvic tissue. The softening of the connective tissue, triggered by hormones, prepares the pelvic tissue, which will have to stretch during the birth. Immediately before the birth, the mare's flanks collapse slightly. This is caused by the foal's changing position in the uterus. Throughout the pregnancy the foal lies with its back downwards or to the side; when labour sets in, it turns on to its belly, its head lying on its legs and facing the cervix. Birth is imminent when the mare begins to become restless. At short intervals, she lies down, rolls, stands up again, paws the ground and carefully smells the place on which she was lying. She often looks back at her body and licks her belly. After the first contractions she lies down. The contractions push the limbs of the foal towards the cervix, thus widening it from the inside. The whitish-blue amniotic sac, which enclosed the foal in the uterus, breaks, allowing the amniotic fluid to escape. The pressure which the foal exerts on the walls of the birth canal increases the contractions which are supported by the contraction of the abdominal muscles. These muscular contractions are most effective when the mare is lying down. She lies flat on her side and stretches her uppermost rear leg so that it does not touch the ground. The foal's forelegs leave the uterus first, followed by the head, which acts as a wedge, allowing the shoulders to escape. The foal is still covered by the amniotic sac, which tears as a result of the pressure exerted on it or through nodding movements of the foal's head. The foal then takes its first breath. The birth takes an average of about 18 minutes. Mares giving birth for the first time usually take longer, even though their foals weigh less at birth than that of a mare who has given birth before. Exhausted, the mother lies on the ground. Her foal, wet and with drooping ears, is still lying in the amniotic sac. Its rear legs have not yet fully escaped. Its front hooves have soft, white pads on the undersides, which prevent damage to the mare's uterus and cervix during birth. This soft bone will soon fall off and the hooves will harden. The foal's

After a final contraction the whole body of the foal, apart from the hind legs, has been born.

The mother touches her newborn for the first time. It is wet, has drooping ears and is still lying in its amniotic sac. An older foal from the same group also greets the new arrival.

first breaths drastically increase the concentration of oxygen in its blood, giving the baby animal sufficient energy to move. When it has finally pulled itself free, it collects its legs under its belly and, with enormous effort, attempts to stand. To do so, it has to bend its hind legs and position them under its belly, while simultaneously stretching its front legs – a difficult task! As soon as the front end is up, the hind legs begin to wobble and collapse, and vice versa.

Meanwhile, the mare has stood up and, in the process, torn the umbilical cord at a place naturally designed for that purpose. She touches her newborn and carefully smells the amniotic sac and the ground. However, she neither eats the sac nor, later, the placenta. Nor does she help her foal to free itself from the amniotic sac; she merely touches and licks it, which encourages it to make further attempts at getting up. The intensive licking stimulates the foal's circulation and frees it of the amniotic fluid. It also helps the mare to familiarize herself with the smell of the foal. From now on, she alone will accept and mother only this foal. Adoption by another mare is unheard of in the wild.

The importance of smell in recognizing and accepting the newborn is illustrated by the example of two Camargue mares, whose behaviour stands in complete contrast with that of other mothering mares. Both mares gave birth

While the foal makes its first attempts to stand, its mother familiarizes herself with its scent.

to a foal in the same place within two hours of each other. Because each of them touched and licked the other mare's foal, both accepted both foals as their own. For three days after their birth, the foals were able to suckle both mares; however, after that, the mares appeared to be able to recognize the smell of their own foals and chased the other one away.

Through the foal's repeated attempts to get up, the amniotic sac slides off it. Eventually it manages to stand on all fours for a moment, before falling down again. It tries again – and finally stands, albeit very shakily and with its legs wide apart. Only 15 to 40 minutes have passed since its birth! Standing like this, it has more in common with a grasshopper than a horse. To keep its balance, it locks its front legs against the ground with the result that its first steps are likely to be taken backwards. Then it begins, slowly and shakily, to edge its way along the body of its mother, never breaking contact with her. Almost immediately, the foal is presented with the next problem – it has to find the udder. It looks in dark places that offer resistance to its mouth: between its mother's neck and chest or at the top of her legs. The mare stands still, occasionally touching the foal and perhaps nudging it towards her rear legs, where the udder is located. When it stands in the correct position for suckling – parallel to the mare – she nibbles and licks it more intensively. The foal stretches out its tongue and bends the edges upwards to form a channel. After many attempts, which take around 30 to 60 minutes, it finally finds the udder and suckles for the first time. This first nourishment, called colostrum, contains special proteins called antibodies, which protect the foal from certain infections. These are necessary as the newborn foal has no immune system of its own. As these antibodies can be absorbed through the walls of the stomach and intestines for only a short time after birth, it is of great importance that the foal suckles shortly after standing up. A delay of only a few hours can considerably reduce the level of immunization. After about two hours, the foal excretes the meconium, faeces that have collected in the bowels of the foetus.

With the first suckling, the mare not only ensures her foal's survival by securing its nourishment, but her behaviour guarantees its security and comfort.

OVERLEAF
Mothers do not let any other animal near the foal on its first day. This thoroughbred Arab from the Beeghum stud farm in Austria is fending off a young stallion who is a little bit too nosy.

THE FIRST DAY

O n its first day, the foal suckles, cautiously tries to run, sleeps and explores its surroundings. Although it is now looking for milk in the right place, it does not always find it instantly. With every attempt, however, it becomes more adept, until it finally finds the teats at the first try. As soon as it has taken one of them into its mouth, it pushes the udder with its head to stimulate the flow of milk. A first-time mother may occasionally appear surprised to find a little creature at her side. Sometimes, perhaps due to lack of experience or because her udder hurts when it is touched, she fends off her foal's first attempts to suckle. Generally speaking, a foal does not benefit from being the first-born. An inexperienced mother may not be able to protect it from injury when stallions are fighting over her. There is also the danger that she will not offer sufficient resistance a bachelor trying to take her and will go with him, deserting her newborn. On several occasions, a mare has travelled on with her harem, leaving her sleeping foal behind. These were always mares who had given birth for the first time and in their own families. As they spent their entire pregnancy with members of their families, perhaps their ties with their own mothers

ABOVE
Young foals are interested in everything that is around them. (Thoroughbred foal from the Beeghum stud farm.)

were still too great, or the ties with their foals had not yet developed sufficiently. A separation of only a few hours can lead to the mother's rejecting her foal. Lost or deserted foals have little chance of survival in the wild.

Not long after giving birth, the mother begins to graze again, frequently interrupting her feeding to touch her foal. While she eats, her baby explores its surroundings. It approaches strange objects, such as trees, shrubs and

Even on its first day the foal precariously gallops around its mother.

stones, and sniffs and nibbles them without fear. It takes leaves or small twigs into its mouth, shakes its head up and down and throws them up in the air. It already knows how to rub itself against a tree, the ground or its mother's body and how to scratch its own coat with its mouth. It can yawn and make its insecurity known with a distinctive facial expression. Shaking can still cause it to lose its balance and when its mother touches it, it sometimes falls over. If it tries to scratch itself with one of its hind hooves, it usually topples over. Even if it can manage to balance on three legs, the lack co-ordination between its leg and its head prevents it from scratching successfully. It merely waves its leg in the air to no avail.

This foal does not know the world yet, but its ears show that it wants to find out.

A foal often touches its mother and already plays with her on the first day of its life. It bucks and kicks, jumps up on her side or back when she is lying down, pinches her head or nibbles her mane. The mare patiently stays still or continues to graze. The first gallop takes place around the mother, no more than five metres (16 ft) from her. When she moves off, the foal runs beside her close to her head. If it cannot keep up, its mother waits or goes back to it. She walks around it and past it, encouraging it to follow her again. Confronted by obstacles, such as a ditch or a gap in the undergrowth, it often hesitates and stands still. If, despite encouragement from its mother, it does not dare to continue, the mother returns. If, after repeated attempts, it will still not follow her, she looks for a different route.

When the foal sleeps, the mare grazes close by. Any animal approaching her foal attracts her attention. Out of curiosity, it seems, the other members of the harem want to touch and smell the new baby. Yearlings are particularly interested, staring at the small animal again and again. The mare, however, thwarts any attempt by a stranger to make contact with her foal on the first day. She instantly intercepts and kicks any animal that tries to approach her young. This may be because it is vital that the foal familiarizes itself with its mother to prevent the possibility of its following another animal. A newborn foal would follow any large moving thing – another mare, a yearling, even a human being. Only on the second day is it able to recognize its mother, by smell and not yet by sight.

The foal could also be threatened by an animal which it approached. As it does not yet understand threatening gestures, it could receive a painful bite or kick. Young animals are more tolerant, showing a friendly curiosity towards it, but the mother has to keep higher-ranking mares at bay. Since these will, in general, reply with threatening behaviour and refuse to leave, the mother has no choice but to lead her foal away. She threatens and even bites animals with whom she normally has a friendly relationship, such as her yearling or her grooming partner. Even though she does not completely isolate herself, she avoids contact with all other animals on the first day of her offspring's life.

OVERLEAF
The smallest sign of danger causes this mare from the Beeghum stud farm to flee. Her foal, just a few hours old, stays close by her side.

LEFT
Shortly after
giving birth, the
mare begins to
graze again. After
all, she now has to
sustain her foal as
well as herself.

While the mother
affectionately
nibbles her foal, she
moves one hind leg
back slightly to make
her udder more
accessible.

On the first day the mother eats noticeably less than she does on the following days. She has to stand still for suckling, keep other horses away and follow her foal whenever it strays from her side. On the second day, she finds more time to feed. After all, she now has to provide for her offspring as well as herself. In the wild, mares with very young foals are nervous, fleeing at the slightest sign of danger, their foals following at their sides. However, they do not hesitate to attack predators. Zebra mares with foals have frequently been observed using their hooves and teeth to attack hyenas. Naturally, they were supported by the leading stallion, who never lost sight of his mare while she gave birth, and, indeed, had hardly moved from her side since.

OVERLEAF
Even though this
Lippizaner foal in
Hungary is older, it
never strays too far
from its mother,
who is the centre of
its life.

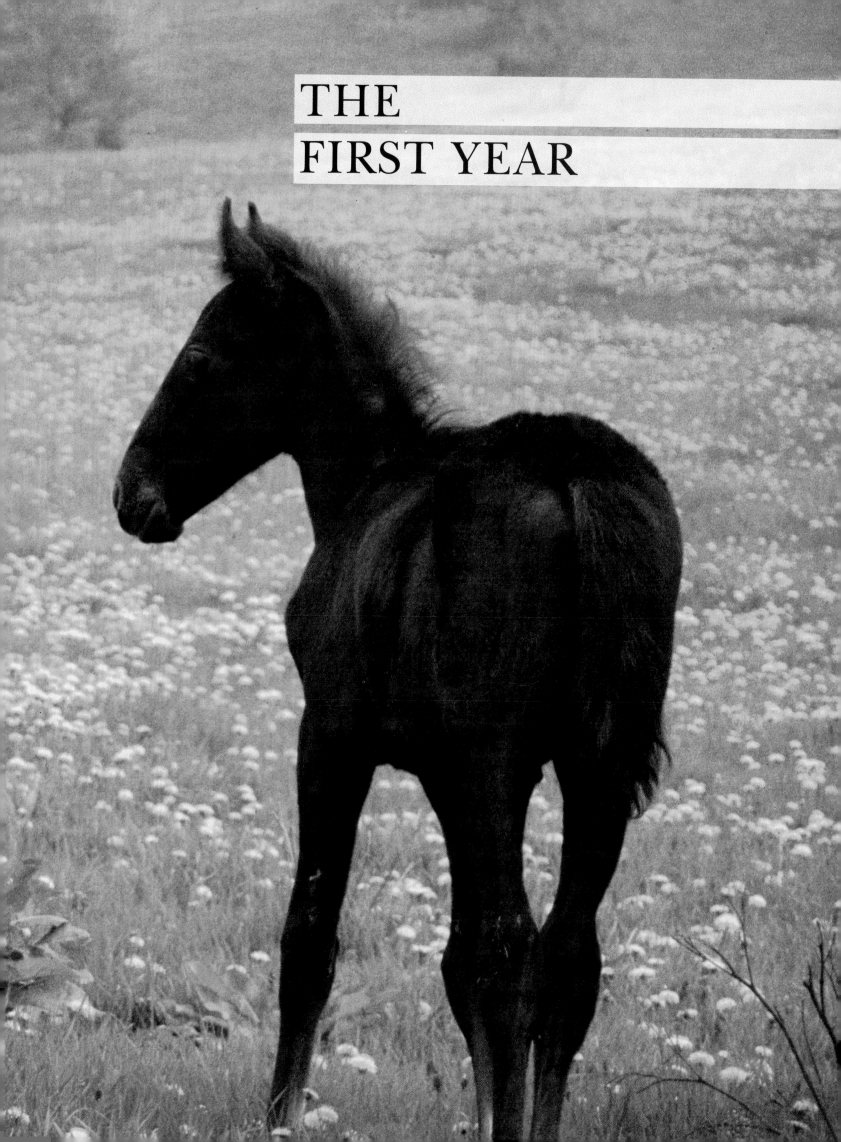

THE
FIRST YEAR

Horses are among those animals whose young follow their mother as soon as they are born and remain in close contact with her at all times. They are distinct from other hoofed animals who leave their young in well-hidden places, only occasionally returning to feed them. Animals that live in the steppe, such as wildebeest and zebra, have to be able to travel to other areas in search of food during the dry season. A young animal, therefore, has to be able to follow its mother and keep up with her so that the whole family can travel over the long distances necessary. In addition, the close proximity of the mother offers the foal protection from predators.

A foal lies flat on the ground to sleep. Its mother stays close by, grazing in a circle around it, or stands beside it to rest. Her foal has to be at least eight weeks old before a mare will go farther off to graze with the other animals of her family in the usual way. In these circumstances, the foal wakes up to find itself alone or surrounded by strange horses. It raises its head and calls for its mother, who replies from the distance. It runs in the direction from which the call came and stops by the nearest mare.

Spring in Spain – a beautiful day for this Hispano-Anglo-Arab foal to race about in this meadow.

Hesitantly it approaches her, but her laid-back ears and swishing tail tell it that this is not one it is looking for. Another whinny from its mother indicates the right direction and it races towards her. By pushing itself under her neck, it forces her to stop; it rubs its head under her belly and, without hesitation, begins to suckle. The mother gives easier access to her udder by stepping back with her rear leg on the foal's side. She does not move away until the foal has finished. The mother is only this considerate of her foal's needs as long as it is

This Haflinger foal has jumped upon its mother, who is its first playmate.

fully dependent on her milk for its nutrition. To begin with, the milk is of exactly the right composition to provides the foal with sufficient nutrition. It drinks 150-250 ml (5-8 fl oz) about twice every hour. However, after a few weeks, the milk is no longer of sufficient quality or quantity and the foal learns to feed itself by copying the other animals. Although it already nibbles at herbs, grass and twigs on the first day of its life, it does not swallow vegetable food until the end of the first week, when its teeth have grown through the gums. To be able to reach the grass, it has to spread its legs apart, which, at the age of four months, is difficult – even for only 15 minutes a day. Older foals often still try to get to the udder. Sometimes both parties become downright insistent; if the foal pushes itself under its mother's neck, she pushes it aside and walks on. When it finally gets to the udder, the mother decides when it should stop suckling by raising her rear leg and running off. Foals become agitated by this premature termination of their feeding and react by laying back their ears and angrily bucking and kicking.

At mother's side the world can be explored in safety.

In its first month, a foal frequently eats its mother's fresh dung. This behaviour is by no means abnormal and has sound physiological reasons. The dung provides the foal with vitamins and single cell micro-organisms, which are vital for the normal functioning of its bowels. By the time it reaches three to four months, a foal will eat almost the same grasses and herbs as adult horses, although it spends nowhere near the same amount of time grazing. Milk still provides much of its nutritional requirements, although the quantity produced by the mare reduces after three or four months. This leaves the young animals more time for playing and sleeping.

As it becomes older, a foal sleeps on its side less often. Instead, it lies on its belly or dozes standing up. In order not to lose its mother, the foal now follows her with 'reeling' steps at short intervals. The responsibility for not getting lost is now the foal's. The mare will follow her young to lead it back to the family when necessary only for the first few days. After that, she tolerates separation over quite large distances, no longer showing concern every time the foal falls behind. Even though it sometimes mistakes a strange mare of similar size and colour for its mother, it is now capable of recognizing her on sight from some distance, and by her smell close by.

Apparently without any reason, a foal may suddenly start to run, stop abruptly and then gallop in a large circle around its mother. Experienced mothers continue to graze, merely following their offspring with their eyes. A young mother, on the other hand, is likely follow it and may intrude upon strange families, causing considerable excitement. Her stallion immediately tries to drive her back to his other mares, meets a neighbour who tries to herd his own agitated mares together, and finally the other foals catch on to the

OVERLEAF
The foal's mother offers not only milk, but also safety. (Arab in Andalusia.)

excitement and start to run around excitedly. It takes a while and many calls from concerned mothers before each foal is back where it belongs.

Naturally, foals rank at the very bottom in the hierarchy. If they encounter adults, they are threatened or kicked, but it seems that older animals show consideration for the inexperience of the youngster. A kick from the hind legs is usually executed with little force – almost as gesture. The foals, on their part, enjoy a kind of fools' freedom. While adult animals respect their superiors and rarely dare to show aggression towards them, foals will direct their threatening gestures at older, more dominant horses. However, their threatening gestures, usually bucking and kicking, are mainly defensive and are not otherwise taken seriously; if they are, mother's social position provides due respect.

A foal observes with interest how its mother paws the sand, lies down and rolls. Even on its first attempt to copy her, it learns the benefits of a dustbath. Despite repeated attempts, however, it is unable, at first, to roll over on to its other side. It has to get up and lie down again to be able to rub both sides on the ground. Meanwhile, the others impatiently await their turn. If an animal pushes in, it is threatened or kicked by the foal. It feels triumphant about making the others wait, but this is really the work of its mother, who has signalled them to wait until her colt or filly has finished. It is, of course, advantageous to have a high-ranking mother; it enables her to offer it privileges such as this. Older foals can mingle with other members of the group without the direct protection of their mothers. On approaching another animal, a foal indicates its insecurity with a chewing gesture. If it is threatened, it reacts with the same expression. This, it seems, prevents stronger action if the foal does not immediately obey a higher ranking horse

Its mother is the centre of a foal's life. She offers protection and she provides food. From her side begin its little explorations, and at her side it learns to run. It is hardly surprising, therefore, that she is also its first playmate.

Foals have a lot of time to laze around, play and, above all, sleep.(Lippizaner foal in Hungary.)

OVERLEAF
As long as the foal is still small, its mother, a Camargue mare, always stays close by, even when it is asleep.

BROTHERS & SISTERS One

morning some time in spring, the young horse, by now a year old, suddenly finds a young creature at its mother's side. Surprised and curious, it approaches its new sibling to touch and smell it, but the mother blocks its path and chases it off with a painful bite. This happens every time it tries to make contact with the foal. She even shows aggression when it wants to approach or touch her. Luckily, this behaviour – inexplicable and frightening to the yearling but vital for the protection of the newborn – does not last too long. Under the careful supervision of its mother, it is allowed to touch the foal on the second day. As the days go by, the mare gradually lets the yearling approach her again and their relationship returns to its normal state. The yearling will still rest beside her, run to her when danger threatens and follow her when she walks off. However, the first place behind her is now occupied by the foal. The first meeting with the foal, too, holds a surprise for the yearling: the foal evades it and presses itself against its mother's belly and even kicks at it. If,

On excursions the foal is always the first in line behind its mother, followed by older brothers or sisters. (Family of Andalusians in Spain.)

94

however, the foal mistakes it for their mother and searches for the udder under its belly, it gets a friendly sniffing from the yearling.

Within a few days the foal grows used to the presence of its older brother or sister. Its curiosity often leads it to the yearling, whose friendly behaviour encourages increasing contact between the two. The little foal is particularly welcome when it shows a willingness to join in with social grooming activities.

After the first four weeks, the foal is at the side of its mother for only half the time, spending the rest of the day with its brothers or sisters, who are the first animals, apart from its mother, that it gets to know. Only then, does it make contact with its contemporaries. The more independence the foal gains from its mother, the closer its relationship with its siblings becomes. The yearling is now rarely chased off by its mother – usually only when the foal needs to suckle. She, presumably, does this to let her yearling know that the milk is exclusively for the foal. Nevertheless, it is said that exceptions prove the rule – some yearlings manage to trick their mothers and sometimes get to the udder by, for example reaching the teats through the mare's hind legs. In the case of a one-eyed Camargue mare, her yearling was able to suckle by approaching her on her blind side. These tactics are generally only successful when the foal suckles at the same time or when the mother is dozing or not paying attention. It is rare for the 'thief' to profit for long. Maybe its better developed teeth or the way in which it takes the teats into its mouth give the game away.

The bond between mother and offspring breaks only when the child leaves the family. (Thoroughbred Arab mare with foal and older daughter on the Beeghum stud farm, Austria.)

The company of its sibling furthers the foal's independence from its mother. It dares to leave her side at an earlier age than foals without siblings. By late autumn, the foal will spend as much time and have as much social contact with its brother or sister as it will with its mother. The arrival of yet another foal strengthens the bond between the two older ones even more. These friendships can become so close that, when the oldest offspring leaves the family, the next oldest follows it. Conversely, a yearling will not feel inclined to leave its mother if she does not give birth again or her new foal dies early in life.

PLAYMATES

At first the mare decides with whom her young is allowed to have contact. Initially, the foal itself runs from unknown animals and hides behind its mother. However, in order to fit successfully into the social structure of the family and the herd, it is essential that it gets to know the other members of the family. The preconditions for this are a lessening degree of maternal protection and an increase in the foal's confidence. Initially, it leaves its mother for only short intervals. Gradually it goes farther afield and leaves her for longer periods of time. Adult animals usually chase it away, but other foals welcome its presence. They form groups which graze, lie down and, most of all, play together. Differences between colts and fillies become apparent at an early age. While fillies take part in chases, they hardly ever fight with each other and only occasionally fight with colts. As fillies' involvement is somewhat passive, colts seek each others' company when they want to play. At only ten days old, they are already grabbing each other's necks with their teeth, playfully biting each other's legs, rearing and chasing each other to bite each other's croup. They strike out with fore and hind legs, suddenly fleeing only to return to confront their playmates again. The same behaviour – only rougher and resulting in a few scratches – can later be observed among young stallions. The early parts of the morning and evening are the usual times for play. A journey to the watering hole, another pasture or a resting place usually encourages play. After a prolonged period of playing, the foals usually return to their mothers, suckle and then, exhausted, fall to the ground and sleep. The older they get the more time they spend with their playmates, also grazing together. Nevertheless, when they want to rest, they still return to members of their families, preferring to sleep next to their mothers.

It is now autumn and the foal has grown. Its coat has lost its smooth appearance and is now thick and shaggy. It no longer has disproportionately long legs compared with the length of its body. Its muscles have developed through play and its rump has become wider. It can now confidently move about its herd and also knows other youngsters of the same age and older, as well as the members of its own family. The time has come to start out on the road to adulthood. The end of its childhood is signified by an event which is very unpleasant for the foal – being weaned off its mother's milk.

Only male foals play this energetically. (Haflinger foals in the Tyrol.)

LEFT
The older the foals become, the more important playmates are to them. (Young Dülmener in Germany.)

OVERLEAF
Biting the cheeks and legs is all part of the game between these Haflinger foals in Vorarlberg, Austria.

WEANING

As it gets older, the foal has an increasing number of unpleasant experiences; now, as soon as it approaches its mother's udder, it is threatened by her, even bitten. To rest or graze beside her is still permitted, but any attempt to touch her is rebuffed. Occasionally, it succeeds in procuring a small sip of milk from her udder, which, by now, is almost dry. The foal is about to experience its first conflict with its mother. All its attempts, even its bucking and kicking, are in vain – no more milk. The youngster now has to find its own nourishment. The highly nutritious protein it received in the milk is now missing from its diet and, at the age of eight months, it is in the middle of a period of rapid growth. To obtain the required nourishment and to reach half the bodyweight of an adult in the next four to six months, it has to find a lot of time for grazing – between 14 and 18 hours, depending on the quality of the food available. This is the same length of time as older, bigger horses. This means less time for sleeping, lazing around and playing with its companions. It gradually distances itself from its mother and spends much of its time grazing with other foals, who share the same fate. Its relationships with other animals, and especially the proximity of its mother, whose friendly contact is now increasing again, help him through this difficult time.

For orphaned foals life is harder. They may be seen standing at the edge, lonely and lost, leaning against a tree as if to draw comfort from it. Sometimes they even refuse to feed during the day. In natural herds homeless foals sometimes find 'foster mothers', usually relatives, such as an older sister or brother.

At the other extreme, there are comparatively fortunate foals, who are allowed to suckle for as long as eight months. This happens when the mare does not become pregnant the following spring and sometimes when the foal is the first born. In the former case, the foal may have the benefit of its mother's milk until it is 18 months old. Whether the mare is covered in the following year is of no significance – two years is the limit in any case. If the mare has given birth for the first time, the suckling period is extended for a further two months; a precious bonus for the foal, considering the lack of good quality fodder in the wild during the winter months. The grass not only lacks protein, but it is also dry. At least it fills the stomach; during that time, the foal's belly is often the only round part of its body. Cold nights, an early winter and a thick layer of snow stretch the foal's resources as much as poor quality food and the lack of vitamins, which restrict skeletal growth. Even the cuddly appearance of the foal, lent to it by its thick winter coat, cannot hide the fact that the first winter decides not just its physical development, but its very survival.

A hard time
begins for this
Dülmener now
that he has been
weaned.

EARLY ADULTHOOD

After a hard winter, the arrival of spring is heralded by the lengthening days. At last there is sufficient grass again. To shed their winter coats, the animals rub themselves against trees and roll on the ground at every opportunity. Difficult-to-reach areas, such as the withers, the back and the croup, are freed of itching hair with the help of others. The young animals, by now a year old, generally choose grooming partners of their own age and take up their favourite pastime again – playing.

The difference between mares and stallions at play, already established at a younger age, becomes more apparent. Female yearlings may spend time with their younger siblings, but their activities can hardly be described as playing. They rub their heads on the foal's body, put it on their backs and with their chests push it along in front of them. The foals hardly respond to this 'game'. By contrast, the play of the stallions becomes even more energetic and intensive. Within their age group, grooming and playing are not the only activities, however; fights also break out. Instead of bucking and kicking – a mode of behaviour, incidentally, still shown towards older animals – they threaten and bite each other. A hierarchy of rank is in the process of being established, but, at this stage, it is by no means permanently fixed. Here, a difference between the sexes becomes apparent: young mares appear, at least at this age, to dominate their male contemporaries. The only animals certain to show submissive behaviour towards a yearling stallion are foals.

A male yearling still has close links with his mother, but shows increasing interest in his father. He often seek his father's company, showing his respect with a typical submissive expression. The stallion appears to have no interest in his son, although sometimes they groom each other or the yearling manages to encourage him to play a game. Yearling stallions show a greater interest in

In bachelor groups, fights to establish rank and hierarchy take place as well as 'playfights'. Threatening gestures, such as the one from this Arab stallion, are serious.

their fathers than young mares demonstrate. Mares and stallions play very different roles later in life. It makes sense, therefore, that their development in the second year of their lives follows different paths. They do have one thing in common, however: life becomes serious when they leave their families.

Most animals, besides young horses, leave their families, some of them long before their bodies are fully developed. These include prairie zebras, the young of the South American camel, guanacos and vicuñas. There are good reasons for this early departure from the familiar family. The adult males of all of these hoofed animals stay with their females all year round, defending them against other males. Their growing sons are, therefore, potential rivals although, as we will see later, they usually leave the arena of their own volition. In addition, remaining in the family can lead to inbreeding. Mating of close relatives – mother and son, for example – may result in weaker, less healthy offspring. This is equally true for daughter and father pairings, which could, genetically, have undesirable consequences.

Furthermore, if all daughters remained in the family, a shortage of food might result, which would, much to the detriment of the whole group, lead to increased rivalry among the mares. Not only the weakest would feel the pinch. The mares would frequently get in each other's way and would, consequently, not have much time to feed in peace. An increase in the size of his harem to this extent would make it much more difficult for the stallion to control and keep his group together. The risk of a mare falling behind and being taken by another stallion would also be greatly increased. All in all, enough reasons for animals to leave of their own accord – although young camels are not that considerate and have to be driven away by their fathers!

Until recently, little was known about young mares. Their development is more subtle than that of their male counterparts. Recent research, however, has shown that their lives are just as fascinating and that their path to adulthood may lead them in different directions.

THE YOUNG MARE

The physical development of the horse is by no means complete in two years. Although the rate of growth reduces in the second year, a horse is not fully grown until it is four or five. Ponies, primitive species and Camargue horses take as long as six or seven years to reach their final size. In terms of their social behaviour, however, mares are grown up long before they reach this age. Adulthood means motherhood and membership of a harem and mares are able to give birth at the age of two. As a rule, however, mares in natural herds do not begin to reproduce until the third year of their lives and wild horses, such as Mustangs, not until the age of four. Mares have their first fertile periods when they are 18 months old, although these are irregular and of short duration. Because they are not yet fully mature, the behaviour of the young mares in their first oestrus is not always recognizable as such and the period may pass almost unnoticed. They do not attract the same sort of attention that a fully grown mare receives from a stallion. If a mare mates during this time, it will be with a stallion of the same age, either from her own or from another group. Leading stallions from other groups also sometimes copulate with these mares, without taking them into their own groups afterwards. Her father pays little attention to the young mare. He makes no attempt to prevent other stallions from approaching her and does not take a stand against rivals, provided they maintain a respectful distance from his own mares. The young mare herself shows an unwillingness to pair with him, evading his attempts to approach her and showing her submissive expression.

Young mares often remain at the edge of the group. When they are on heat they go off to visit other harems. (Haflinger mares in the Tyrol.)

The first heat of a mare in her 'teenage years', therefore, rarely leads to pregnancy. The situation changes when the cycle commences the following spring. Whether it takes place at the first occurrence or after several cycles, the first time a young mare is covered is usually successful. In many cases, this event coincides with her departure from her family. The first signs of her impending departure become apparent some time before she finally leaves. She seeks less contact with her mother, who tolerates her presence without either paying much attention to her or chasing her away. A young mare often stays at the edge of her original harem, sometimes leaving her group for several hours, even days. She visits other harems, preferring those with other young animals. She keeps returning to her own family until, one day, she stays with the group of her choice. As the young mare is on heat at that time, she is covered by the

male members of their new group – the young stallions as well as the leading stallion. However, her integration takes time. The older mares are aggressive towards the newcomer, who is forced to take the lowest position in the hierarchy. The leading stallion does not pay much attention to her once she is no longer on heat; several weeks pass before he recognizes her as a member of his group and defends her from other stallions. Her choice of suitable partners is, therefore, limited to other young animals, in general mares, with whom she forms close links.

Some young mares take a different direction. They allow strange stallions to cover them – usually several different ones – without moving to another group. These mares spend a further 11 months with their families, by the side of their mothers and siblings. Their situation is finally changed irreversibly and dramatically with the birth of their first foal. Young bachelors, who have waited for an opportunity such as this, or older stallions intending to increase the size of their harems throw themselves at such a mare and try to take her with them. Whether her new owner will be a bachelor or a leading stallion is decided not by her, but by the outcome of a battle between the stallions.

Observing and understanding young mares takes patience, as their behaviour is inconspicuous. (Haflinger mare in the Tyrol.)

Whichever way a mare becomes a member of a new harem, she will be with that group for a long time, if not her entire life. If the stallion dies or is replaced by a younger stallion, the mares stay together and are taken over as a group by their new owner. Depending on conditions, she will give birth every year – and leave her growing daughters to go their own way.

THE YOUNG STALLION

Like mares, stallions grow slowly. Although they are physically capable of covering a mare at the age of two years, their career as successful parents begins later in life. Most stallions do not father a foal until they are five years old, by which time a mare of the same age will have given birth several times. In ideal conditions, mares can give birth every spring until they are 20 years old. The reproductive success of a stallion is not so predictable. Though they can cover several mares in any one year, the number of foals they father in a lifetime depends on factors such as the size and quality of their surroundings, the size of their harem, their ability to compete and the age at which they form their harem. A stallion will father most of his foals between the ages of nine and 11; after that the number reduces. However, as some stallions are very successful at that age, while others have a limited number of descendants and a few father no foals at all, this can be viewed only as a generalization.

Regardless of how old he is when he has the first mare of his own, how many he will have and how long he will be able to maintain his position as leading stallion, a bachelor's adulthood begins, as it does for a mare, when he leaves his family. The most likely reason for his leaving is prevention of incest. A direct reason for his departure is the change in relationship with his father. The fact that a young stallion will move on even if the leading stallion is not his genetic father supports the assumption that social mechanisms rather than genetic recognition of relatives are operating. The few cases of a brother copulating with his sister may be explained by the fact that the older brother had replaced the leading stallion of the harem of which his sister was a member; as he had left by the time she was born, he could not have known her. In the wild, such incidences are probably extremely rare because young stallions tend to travel a greater distance when they leave their families than young mares. A meeting with a relative is, therefore, a rare coincidence.

This group of bachelors would play just as vigorously in the wild. (Ponies in Germany.)

As the leading stallion becomes increasingly annoyed by the presence of his son, his threatening gestures increase. Sometimes he will attack the younger horse, despite its submissive expression. No young stallion can stand up to such an attack. He takes flight, closely pursued by the older animal, whose laid-back ears show that this is no game. In general, young stallions do not let it come to that, choosing, instead, to escape the growing tension in their family. The other reason for a young stallion to leave his family is almost certainly his desire to find contemporary companions. In the wild, young stallions some-times travel great distances in search of a new group. They are welcomed by other stallions who share the same fate – into so-called bachelor groups.

Bachelor groups comprise not only young stallions, but also former leading stallions who have been defeated and replaced or whose mares have died. A constant coming and going takes place in these groups; older animals leave the group to form a harem and are replaced by younger ones. Young stallions usually spend one or two years with a bachelor group; some stay longer. Close one-to-one friendships are sometimes formed, usually between animals who already knew each other perhaps having come from the same group. All mem-bers of a bachelor group have a friendly relationship with each other. They graze together peacefully, clean each other's coats and, above all, play a lot.

Another popular pastime among young stallions is demonstrating rank. Despite their friendship, there is a certain degree of rivalry, although fights will only break out once the stallions have started to look for mares.

Then, one day in spring, a mare gives birth – an opportunity for an older bachelor! Stallions who try to conquer a mare in pairs are no exception. If the attempt is successful, controlled conditions will exist in the new family. One of them is superior to the other and asserts himself by being the last one to deposit his dung on any heap. Apart from that, the role of each individual ani-mal is clearly defined; when a rival threatens, the subordinate stallion faces him, while the other brings the mare into safety. Only the dominant stallion has the right to copulate with her – or so one would assume – but it appears that the inferior stallion also fathers a foal with this mare from time to time.

This relationship does not always stand up to the constant pressures within it; demonstration of rank leads to fights and the weaker animal may eventually decide to leave. If the harem has, through successful co-operation, increased in size, the departing animal usually takes the lowest-ranking mare with him. So the stallion has reached his goal – to own one or two mares with whom he will be able to spend many peaceful years.

OVERLEAF
Young Lippizaner
stallions in a playful
chase.

HORSE-PLAY & COMBAT

In the course of playing at fighting, almost all of the techniques of serious combat are used – but with less vigour. Two stallions playfully begin to bite each other's cheeks, before aiming for the legs, neck and head. To avoid being bitten, they dodge their opponent and circle around him, or they simply place their rumps on the ground. To protect their forelegs they kneel. Now and again, to evade their opponent's attacks or to come down on top of him, they rear. This is followed by a chase, during which the animal being chased suddenly stops, wheels around and attacks and chases his pursuer. The intensity of play is indicated by the position of the ears and the facial expression: younger stallions play with their ears pointing forwards or sideways and their faces are relaxed, while older animals tend to lay their ears back and tense their facial muscles. 'Playfights' between older stallions can end up as serious conflict, particularly in spring. Numerous bruises are inflicted and, occasionally, one animal is lamed; this gives an indication of the intensity of these tussles. The stallions are, it seems, in a heightened state of excitement. It is now known that, in spring, a stallion's bloodstream contains a higher concentration of testosterone, a male sexual hormone, than it does in autumn or winter.

Playing at fighting is training for the real event. Bites to the opponent's head and neck and rapid turns followed by kicks can decide the outcome of a fight in seconds. (Young Lippizaner stallions.)

Like many other mammals, stallions play in order to practise their fighting tactics, getting to know their future rivals' strengths and weaknesses at the same time. This experience probably better enables them to determine the risk of losing a real battle and incurring injury. To distinguish between play and confrontation is not always easy for the casual observer and the transition from the one to the other can be seamless – a harmless scuffle can suddenly escalate into serious combat. Nevertheless, there are clear signs which distinguish play from fighting. A desire to play is indicated by a raised head and repeated nodding at the partner. The ears, although possibly pointing back slightly, are not pressed back against the head. Serious biting is replaced by gentle nipping and rank is of no importance – both animals play the role of the hunter. Apart from heavy breathing, no noise is made during a 'playfight'. Combatant stallions, on the other hand, are reported to have a very loud battle call.

True animosity between stallions may develop gradually. They may meet repeatedly and try to intimidate each other without actually fighting. Then, suddenly and without warning, one of them attacks the other, mouth wide open showing his teeth. The second stallion has no choice but to rear to evade the attack and avoid injury to his head and neck. For a fraction of a second he has the upper hand; he is now in a position to drop his weight on his opponent and try to grab the top of his assailant's head with his teeth. Before he

The risk of death in battle is as small for stallions as the risk of death in giving birth is for a mare. (Lippizaner stallions in Hungary.)

has time to do so, the other stallion also rears. If he is fast enough, he can throw himself between the kicking front legs and grab his opponent's throat. However, if he fears the power of the kicks, the two will now engage in a veritable boxing contest with their front hooves. As they keep their distance from each other, the danger of injury is relatively small. The situation changes when one horse turns and kicks with his hind legs. These kicks are forceful and well aimed, the head and legs of the opponent being the target.

The fight ends as suddenly as it began. If the two separate following a frenzied pawing and posturing, the battle has probably not been decided – they will meet again. The dispute is concluded when one of them realizes the futility of his attempts to gain the upper hand or when one of them beats the other in combat and chases him off. Premature submission benefits a weaker opponent, as these duels hold a high risk of injury. Vulnerable areas, such as the lips and ears, are easily damaged and deep flesh wounds on neck, croup or flank are prone to infection. Broken bones are the most dangerous injury. Broken ribs can heal, but a broken leg or jaw amounts to a death sentence. The rare occurrence of death following a fight shows how well horses are able to judge their own abilities and those of their opponent.

FRIENDSHIP

Throughout their lives horses form friendships with one or two other animals, but their preferred partner changes as they develop. A foal, of course, has a close relationship with its mother. As it becomes older, brothers and sisters become more important to it. Later, having left its family, it builds relationships with its peers. Young stallions prefer other stallions, mares other young mares. Adults stay true to their chosen partners. Only through death, theft of a mare or replacement of a leading stallion can change be forced. For a mare, the cycle is completed when her first foal is born. Her most important partners from now on will always be her stallion

Friendly contact between young Haflinger stallions in the Tyrol.

and her youngest offspring. The development of a stallion is completed when he forms a harem. From now on, his mares are his most important partners. As owner of a harem, the stallion has control over his mares, but ownership is really too strong a word. His relationship with the mares shows the same characteristics as the relationships between young animals and between a mother and her foal. The terms 'friendship', 'faithfulness' and 'chosen partnership' are all a means of saying the same thing – a close relationship between two horses. The most important factor in a relationship such as this is time – time spent together. Never losing sight of one another, day and night, for years on end when they are adults, they while away the time at the side of their friends. Regardless of their activity – grazing, resting or dustbathing – they are never far apart. If they are separated, they call for each other and do not rest until they are together once again. Standing next to each other and rubbing their heads against each other, they fend off irritating insects.

This knowledge enables you, the rider or even the lucky horse-owner, to be your horse's 'chosen partner'. For people to whom the horse has always been more than just a riding animal, the following advice will not be news. Although you may not be aware of it, your intuitive behaviour towards your horse is in keeping with the social rules that horses follow in the wild. In this case, too, much time needs to be spent with the horse to become a partner. A horse living in a natural group does, after all, want to graze with its friends and not alone. Go for walks with the horse on its halter – friendly horses, too, follow each other around. Hold still when it rubs is head against your shoulder: perhaps it does not want to rid itself of a horsefly or its bridle, but is indicating trust and showing that it likes you. Take the place of its horse partner and ruffle its withers or its back. It will understand your intention. If the horse leaves the other grazing animals when it sees you coming, even though you are not holding a piece of sugar, you have won. Its greatest proof of trust would be a siesta at your side. As you know, a friendship is for life and is based on mutual trust. With any luck your friendship with the horse will last a lifetime.

THE HORSE: ANIMAL OF FLIGHT

To survive in the wild, a horse has to be able to run for its life – its only defence against predators is speed. To leave danger behind as quickly as possible it will run. With its short, stiff back, high hocks, relatively inflexible legs, large nostrils allowing a high air intake and an excellent blood supply to the muscles it is perfectly adapted for that purpose. Donkeys, on the other hand, have more flexible legs which improves their ability to cope with mountainous terrain. Horses can see into the distance to look for approaching predators, as well as keeping an eye open in their immediate vicinity to watch their step, avoid obstacles on the ground or to look for food. They see a lot, but they do not necessarily see it clearly.

Horses' eyes are among the largest in the animal kingdom. The distance between retina and lens and the circumference of the retina are also exceptionally large. Their ability to see in low light or at night is far superior to our own. The position of their eyes on the sides of their head, combined with the large circumference of the retina, enables them to see a large proportion of their surroundings. Each eye can capture an angle of 215° horizontally and 178° vertically. Their field of vision overlaps in front of the face by 60-70°, giving them three-dimensional vision in that area.

Despite their ability to see objects in front of, beside and behind them without turning their heads, horses could do with spectacles, because they suffer from astigmatism. The eye's unevenly-shaped lens distorts the image which they see. They correct this fault by slightly lifting their heads until the image of the object is projected on to an area of the retina where it is sharply focused. One area of the retina is specialized for recognizing movement, but, as re-

After thousands of years of domestication, horses still flee at the first sign of danger. (Andalusian stallion in Spain.)

PREVIOUS PAGE
With a powerful gallop this Andalusian stallion tries to climb a sand dune to gain a better view of his surroundings.

focusing from close to distant vision is difficult, a horse will sooner flee at the first sight of an unknown object and determine its nature afterwards. When a predator threatens, the slightest hesitation can lead to death. Sometimes a horse will shy away from an object that seems to be animated, as it appears in and leaves the horse's field of vision through the movement of its own head.

If a horse looks at an object directly in front of it, its surrounding vision is unclear and vice versa. The best and farthest vision is achieved by raising the head and alternately looking ahead and to the side. This posture is adopted when a horse becomes aware of something unusual. The ears move in all directions to identify any noise. If he considers the disturbance worthy of caution, the leading stallion neighs or snorts, which warns the other horses, if his posture has not already alerted them. Nostrils wide open and muscles taut, the stallion takes a few steps towards the cause of his disquiet. Meanwhile, the other members of his group move closer together and position themselves behind him. If the disturbance proves to be harmless, the stallion turns around and the group moves away together. After 50-100 metres (160-325 ft), they stop to observe their surroundings once again. To avoid dissipating their energy needlessly, they adjust their speed according to the nature of the danger. Unknown or seemingly dangerous objects in the distance are evaded at a walking or trotting pace; if they are surprised by a disturbance close by, they flee in a fast gallop, dispersing in all directions in the process. In open terrain, they regroup only after they have gained a safe distance.

The only remaining predators horses have in the wild are pumas and wolves. They will also flee from bears, although these are not their natural adversaries.

Even heavy horses, such as this Frisian stallion, show light-footedness and elegance when galloping.

OVERLEAF
The particularly agile Haflinger horses even enjoy running about in the snow.

Pumas actually hunt deer, but can, like the coyote, present danger to weak, ill or deserted foals. Packs of wolves sometimes hunt even adult horses, but they usually prefer reindeer, bison or domestic cattle.

Compared to horses, zebras lead a more dangerous life; their enemies include hyena, leopards, lions and cheetahs. On open grassland, they often follow the example of antelopes and wildebeest, who share the savanna with them, and flee when they do. Like a horse, a Hartmann or mountain zebra stallion stands between the potential source of danger and his group and is the last to take flight. Like horses, zebra stallions warn their group with a snort – Hartmann zebras also warn with a short, rasping bark. Grevy zebras, whose stable groups consist of only a mother and her foal, stand a better chance of evading an assailant if they form larger herds. A single zebra is easier prey for a lion than a zebra in a larger herd. The huge herds of wildebeest – the preferred sustenance of all the large African predators – provide even more protection for the zebras. If they join the wildebeest, they are less likely to fall prey than they are if they merely form groups with other zebras. Most zebras choose this method of avoiding predators, but have to pay a price. The large numbers of wildebeest eat up to 80 per cent of the available food, of which the zebras, not being ruminants, need more. To compensate for this disadvantage, they stay at the front of the herd where the ground has not yet been grazed. A further problem is posed by the many calves born among the wildebeest during the rainy season; this attracts predators who are also dangerous to them. When food is in short supply at the start of the dry season, the zebras leave the wildebeest to form groups of exclusively their own kind; they no longer compete for food with the wildebeest, but stand an increased risk of falling prey to a hunter. The dry season is particularly dangerous to their foals. In exceptionally dry conditions, the mothers sometimes travel over long distances to the nearest watering hole, only returning hours later. In the meantime, their foals are left behind with other defenceless foals. Predators and a shortage of food can account for a death rate of 70 per cent among the foals of the Grevy zebra during such times.

FACIAL
EXPRESSIONS

Horses are capable of a wide variety of facial expressions, which they combine with a range of postures to communicate with each other. To recognize the individual expressions and to know in which situations they are used enables the observer to understand how the horses relate to each other and to us. When horses meet, we can recognize friendship, superiority, rivalry, protection, caring and much more, both from the way in which they approach each other and from their expressions. Many facial expressions are reflexive; in other words, young animals use them from birth without first having to learn them. Expressions and gestures are usually clear enough to eliminate all ambiguity, leaving no doubt as to their meaning. Nevertheless, misinterpretations do occur. A horse can get a big fright if an animal grazing next to it suddenly swings its head to chase off a horsefly. Even though its ears are not laid back and the swing of the head is not aimed at a specific target, the movement resembles a threatening action. A stamp with the rear leg, again intended to fend off an irritating insect, can also be construed as a threatening action by a nearby horse.

If something attracts a horse's attention, it throws its head in the air and looks, unmoving and with heightened senses, for potential danger. Nostrils flared, it sniffs the air. Horses have an exceptionally well-developed sense of smell. The nostrils lead to a large nose, which separates into many small chambers. The mucous membrane of the nose contains closely packed olfactory cells, which enable the stallion to smell a mare on heat from a distance. Their noses are said to be capable of locating water from far away. If they want to examine a smell in close detail, they fleer, producing a characteristic grimace.

Not a laughing Noriket stallion, but a yawning one. (Dolomites, Italy.)

RIGHT
The faces of these Shagya-Arab mares in Hungary express extreme vigilance.

The nostrils are held close to the source of the scent, then the neck is stretched and the head held high up in the air; at the same time, mouth closed, the upper lip is rolled back until the nostrils are as good as shut. This opens access to the Jacobson organ, which is located at the base of the nasal cavity. The air is inhaled via two blind channels and can, with the help of this organ, be inspected for subtle traces of odour. After this intensive assessment the nose drips. Among adult horses it is usually the stallions who fleer; they do this most frequently during the reproductive season after smelling a mare's urine. Tobacco smoke, the first contact with an unknown food and plants with a particularly strong and potent smell can also invoke fleering.

Although communication is mainly visual, horses also use a variety of sounds to communicate with each other. Horses can hear a wider range of frequencies than humans. Furthermore, their long necks and movable ears enable them not only to hear sounds coming from all directions, but also to pinpoint these fairly accurately. The calls of each horse can be distinguished by its tone, strength and variation of vibration. This enables neighing horses to recognize each other from a distance or without visual contact. Oral communication between social partners, such as stallion and mare, or mare and offspring, are

PREVIOUS PAGE
A hearty yawn often signals the end of the siesta. (Young stallion in the Camargue.)

OVERLEAF
Frisian stallions from the Krefeld stud farm testing scent at a urinating place.

An Arab mare from
Andalusia calling
for her foal.

short, of low frequency and are repeated many times. The greater the distance between the animals, the higher and louder the calls become. They neigh at a familiar horse when it leaves and greet it with a whinny when it returns. During the courtship ritual, stallions grunt, while mares squeal. Squealing is also common among stallions during a demonstration of rank.

Laid-back ears are a threatening gesture. Depending on the strength of the threat, the ears are either just pointed back or pressed right back against the head. At the same time, the nostrils contract, the mouth is pulled back and the facial muscles are tensed. Sometimes the white of the eyes is shown. When an animal opens its mouth and shows its teeth, the threat is to be taken more seriously. If the other horse does not evade, it will be bitten. The threatening face announces a kick from the hind legs. Mares kick more frequently than stallions, who usually approach their opponents head first to attack by biting and rearing. Young stallions sometimes kick as a last resort, before they flee from an older stallion. When a stallion wants to herd his mares together, he makes a threatening face combined with a special posture – he lowers his head almost to the ground, keeping his neck stretched, and moves it from left to right to indicate the direction in which he wants them to go.

With its mouth wide open, teeth exposed and eyes closed, a horse appears to be laughing; but it is, in fact, yawning. Horses usually yawn after a rest or when they have just rolled on the ground. Presumably to wind down, stallions will sometimes yawn after copulating or at the end of a confrontation with a rival stallion.

One of the strangest and most conspicuous expressions is chewing, used mainly by young animals to show their submissiveness. Heads lowered, they open their mouths to show their incisors and move their lower jaws up and down; their legs bend slightly and their tails are drawn between the hind legs. Foals show this face when they are threatened by strange animals. Young stallions adopt this posture when they cross the path of or greet a leading stallion. This demeanour usually achieves the desired effect with adults: their aggression is curtailed or evaporates altogether. Sometimes this posture and expression demonstrate a general apprehension rather than inferiority of rank. Foals often when they are anxious or afraid, for example before an awkward obstacle, such as a water-filled ditch or when they pass strange horses adopt this 'chewing' action.

THANKS

My work on this book, which has taken me 12 years, was supported by many people, to whom I owe my gratitude.

I thank Dr. H.C.W. Georg Olms, President of the International Asil-Club for his help and support with photographic work on his Asil-Arab-Hamasa Stud Farm, and Mrs. Barb Müller for her help on the Hamasa Stud Farm.

I am grateful to Dr. Jaromir Oulehla, Director of the Spanish Riding School in Vienna and the National Lippizaner Stud Farm of Piber for their support of my work. In Hungary, I give special thanks to stud-farm manager Mr. Andor Dallos and the Minister of Forestry and Agriculture, Dr. Janos Ott, as well as to Mr. Ivan Thomka, Mr. Nagy Laszlo and Mr. Czopo Gyula.

My sincerest thanks extend to the family of Doris and Andreas Schmidt from Upper Austria for their help, and to the Tonte family in Vienna. In the Tyrol, my special thanks go to Mr. Otto Schweisgut, Mr. Hannes Schweisgut, Mrs. Ilse Benedetto-Schweisgut, Mr. Reinhold Prandstätter and Mrs. Evelin Swarowski. In Czechoslovakia, I thank Dr. Norbert Zális and Miss Barbora Cihákova (in particular for the photograph on pages 140-1). For help during photography of the Friesan horses, I thank Mr. Bernd Reisgies, Chairman of the German Institute of Breeders and Friends of Friesan Horses, Mr. Hanns-Günther Fröhlich, Mrs. Susanne Rappenecker and Christa and Hans-Joachim Dannenfelser.

In Andalusia, I thank Mr. Miguel Angel Cardenas Osuna for his support of my work, as well as his employees, Mr. Miquel Osuna Saaveda, Mr. Fernando Gago Gorcia and Mr. Juan Manuel Uriquijo Novales; in England, the employees of Chevely Park in Newmarket; in France Dr. Luc Hoffmann – founder of the Biological Station La Tour du Valat – and his associates; further I want to thank for their help Dr. Wolfgang Cranz, Director of the National Stud Farm Marbach and Mr. Andrej Franetic, Director of the Stud Farm of Lipica in the former Yugoslavia. In Weitersfelden, my thanks go to the Diesenreiter family for their constant and sincere support with all the work related to this project.

Lída Jahn-Micek
Weitersfelden, August 1990

A NOTE ABOUT THE PHOTOGRAPHY

I am a Canon-photographer. Ever since I started to work as a photographer, I have used Canon cameras. The following photographic equipment was used for the photography in this book: Cameras: Canon EF, Canon A1 with automatic winding mechanism, Canon T90. Lenses: FD 200mm, Canon FD-Zoom 100-300mm, Canon FD-Zoom 28-85mm. I have used Kodak and Fuji film.

This Asil-Arab stallion fleers after smelling the urine of a mare – a form of behaviour rarely shown by mares.

In 1973, following the suggestion of Professor B. Tschanz (University of Bern), a group of Camargue horses was released on 300 hectares of land on the Tour de Valat estate, which is owned by Dr. L. Hofmann. The aim was to study the behaviour of this herd in natural conditions. Numerous researchers ventured to undertake this painstaking task: P. Duncan, C. Feh, C. Frey-Niggli, B. Michel, A.-M. Monard, E. Murbach, B. Tschanz and S. Wells. All Camargue horses depicted in this book are of that herd, which, incidentally, still exists today. American researchers, having observed wild Mustangs for many years, have also made a sizeable contribution to the understanding of the social behaviour of horses: J. Berger, L. Boyd, D. McCullough, R. Denniston, J. Feist and R. Miller. H. Klingel's work about zebras was continued and developed by J. Ginsberg, E. Joubert, B. Penzhorn and A. Sinclair. They all have contributed to the fascinating insight into the life of horses, which I have tried to describe in this book. My special thanks go to Claudia Feh, who has proof-read the manuscript, and my Camargue horse Juanito, which has chosen me as one of its special partners.

Beatrice Michel

Access for Disabled People to Arts Premises

The Journey Sequence

'Everyone has the right to take part in the artistic and cultural life of the community'

Universal Declaration of Human Rights – Article 27

Access for Disabled People to Arts Premises

THE JOURNEY SEQUENCE

C. Wycliffe Noble
and
Geoffrey Lord

AMSTERDAM • BOSTON • HEIDELBERG • LONDON • NEW YORK • OXFORD
PARIS • SAN DIEGO • SAN FRANCISCO • SINGAPORE • SYDNEY • TOKYO

Architectural Press is an imprint of Elsevier

Architectural
Press

Architectural Press
An imprint of Elsevier
Linacre House, Jordan Hill, Oxford OX2 8DP
200 Wheeler Road, Burlington, MA 01803

First published 2004

Permissions may be sought directly from Elsevier's Science and Technology Rights
Department in Oxford, UK: phone: (+44) (0) 1865 843830; fax: (+44) (0) 1865
853333; e-mail: permissions@elsevier.co.uk. You may also complete your request online via the Elsevier homepage (http://www.elsevier.com), by selecting 'Customer
Support' and then 'Obtaining Permissions'

British Library Cataloguing in Publication Data
A catalogue record for this book is available from the British Library

Library of Congress Cataloguing in Publication Data
A catalogue record for this book is available from the Library of Congress

ISBN 0 7506 5779 0

For information on all Architectural Press publications
visit our website at www.architecturalpress.com

Contents

Joint authors

Architect – C. Wycliffe Noble OBE FRIBA FRSA, a Founder Trustee of ADAPT, has long been a pioneer in access. He was architect to the first Centre for Disabled Students at Selly Oak, Birmingham. He has been access adviser on many historical buildings including the Palace of Westminster, Park House on the Royal Sandringham Estate, Somerset House and the Hong Kong Macau Centre, Beijing.

He received the government recognition 'Award for Good Design in Housing' and the European 'Helios Award for the Adaptation of Heritage Buildings'. He has chaired Committees of the British Standards Institution responsible for the new BS 8300: 2001 'Design of buildings and their approaches to meet the needs of disabled people – Code of Practice'.

His development of the criterion 'The Journey Sequence' used for the assessment of buildings for disabled people has been used nationally and internationally.

Co-author – Geoffrey Lord OBE commenced his career with the Midland Bank, changed to the Probation and After Care Service in 1958, where he established the Selcare Trust, and was appointed Secretary and Treasurer to the Carnegie UK Trust in 1977 until retirement in 1993.

He is MA in Applied Social Studies and Founder of Artlink, Edinburgh and the Lothians, and also in 1989 of 'The Voluntary Arts Network' in the UK.

He was the inspiration and Founder of the ADAPT Trust (Access for Disabled People to Arts Premises Today) and is its Vice President.

He is an Honorary Fellow of the Manchester Metropolitan University and was awarded the OBE for services to charity in 1989.

Foreword
By The Earl of Snowdon GCVO

When the Adapt Trust was initiated in 1989 a target was set to achieve effective access to all major arts and heritage premises by the year 2001.

The Trust has accomplished a great deal in those years and has expanded its initial work of grant-aid to include training programmes, consultancy on access, and an award scheme for best practice.

When I was invited to become President I had some doubts about the merits of an award scheme, believing that venues should not be rewarded for a purpose that I believed should be a duty to be accomplished. I was not emphasising the rights of disabled people but more the responsibilities of owners and managers of premises, and this was following my experience as Chairman of the International Year of Disabled People and long before the Disability Discrimination Act came into operation.

However, I learned that the ADAPT awards scheme was not to reward a venue or its management, but to acknowledge achievement and progress, and to ensure that a financial award had to be used to ensure further action for access at the successful venue. The ADAPT awards have been successful in highlighting good practice and in making the difference between basic access and effective access.

I have enjoyed chairing the judging panels and reading the many applications with their descriptions and diagrams. However, I have to say that I found the standard of photographs submitted was low as though illustrating access was not a priority. The authors have also experienced difficulty in gaining satisfactory photographs to illustrate the several features of physical access.

May I suggest to managers of venues that they should utilise good photographs to publicise their achievements and facilities with displays at the venue to attract more customers.

Has the initial target succeeded? Without a full-scale and costly study it would not be possible to state categorically that all major venues are effectively accessible. Certainly many now are, and if not, owners and managers should be looking to their laurels to ensure that by 2004 they are not opting out of a decision to determine that everyone should have favourable access to an arts and heritage venue of their choice.

This publication is timely and I hope that it will be the stimulus to encourage those that have achieved access for all to do a little more, and those that have not yet come to terms with their responsibilities will seek advice, plan how best to achieve effective access at their public venue and take action.

Surely, access for disabled, older and young people must be today and not tomorrow.

Preface

This book is about the achievements and the solutions that have been incorporated into a variety of buildings within the purpose group of arts premises, galleries, museums, libraries and heritage buildings.

It is a photographic review of how the differing needs of people have been met in alternative design solutions and shows how the conditions to maintain the integrity of historical and heritage buildings have been achieved. This is highlighted by the use of photographs and illustrations with captions to identify the salient points of the design.

The range of requirements for disabled people is disparate and encompasses factors related to mobility, dexterity, sensory and cognitive attainment.

The designer therefore has to be cognisant of the differences when aiming for a universal and design for all approach.

This in no way compromises a functional approach to design, but rather recognises the disabling potential that society has imposed on disabled people and older people by inferring that barriers in design cannot be overcome.

This book is not prescriptive in setting down conditions that have to be met. These are already set down in Standards, Regulations and Recommendations.

Rather, it records what has been accomplished in a creative and imaginative manner allowing the reader to visit buildings, exploring the ways in which complex conditions, not necessarily within an architectural dimension, have been resolved in a project of excellence.

Introduction

'The excellence of every art must consist in the complete accomplishment of its purpose' – is the inscription above the entrance to the Victoria and Albert Museum in London.

This quotation applies equally to the concept of effective access to venues because one has to cultivate an attitude and response, particularly of architects and venue managers, and also of planners and the general public. All of us need to think beyond the constraints of architecture and regulations and expand our vision to meet the aspirations for the social inclusion of people. Thus a whole range of provisions in the field of information technology and communication skills, essential for the sensory impaired and those with cognitive impairments, must be developed and applied.

Since *The Committee of Inquiry into Arts and Disabled People* reported in 1988[1] and the creation of the ADAPT Trust (see Appendix 2) there has been a significant improvement in access at main arts and heritage premises in the UK. However, even now in 2003, many older buildings, even when renovated, and several of the new buildings do not achieve effective access for all people. The obstacles are many and varied, yet it is possible to create access at the majority of public venues, however historic, with imagination and determination.

Aesthetic appeal allied to the nature of the building, and practical considerations allied to effective use and maintenance, must be harnessed together with cost implications. Sometimes the overriding consideration of the historic nature of the building means that a secondary and alternative solution has to be achieved. For example, it may not be possible to alter the main entrance with its many steps, but that need not rule out a satisfactory alternative. Access to an upper floor where impractical in a museum or gallery can be ameliorated by the provision of a video displaying pictures of collections upstairs.

The impossible is nearly always possible given goodwill, good sense and good design, and where a barrier or obstacle is recognised initially, alternatives should be assessed.

Effective access as part of an integral process of good design is beneficial to all consumers not only in arts and heritage premises but also as seen in the retail sector.

Electronically operated doors, lifts, ramps and handrails on stairs are a necessary consideration and for those who, on entering a building, need to locate the position of restrooms, WCs and other facilities.

Good signs, communication systems, provision and location of seats are elements used in 'The Journey Sequence' providing effective access and comfort.

'The Journey Sequence', described on pages 2 and 3, can be applied to any building, but in this book it applies to arts and heritage premises of distinction which are included in the examples selected for this book.

The book is about achievements and the solutions that have been incorporated into a variety of buildings.

The whole is a review of how effective access has been achieved involving sensible and sound design.

The selection of buildings identified those that had achieved distinction in one of the ADAPT awards programmes or within a national award scheme such as those announced annually by The Royal Institute of British Architects.

Some projects, however, were included where a positive, comprehensive policy of accessibility existed within a partnership between the providers, designers, facilities and maintenance managers. This enabled performing arts and the use of facilities in museums and libraries to be kept under review so as to be an enriching experience enjoyed by many people.

This book does not pretend to be a technical journal – there are several listed in the Bibliography – but a descriptive account of interesting venues where management and staff and advisers have cultivated their audience, aimed at excellence and taken action to meet the varying needs of people.

[1] '*Arts and Disabled People*' (The Attenborough Report) 1985 includes the main recommendations of the Committee of Inquiry. Published for the Carnegie UK Trust by Bedford Square Press, London (ISBN 0 7199 1145 1).

Partnership and teamwork

Acknowledgements

To all those who have provided inspiration for us to pursue the objectives of the book:

The ADAPT Trustees
(Access for Disabled People to Arts Premises Today)

The Earl of Snowdon GCVO – President – The ADAPT Trust
Professor Patrick Nuttgens CBE
David Petherick DipArch FRSA
Elizabeth Noble MSc – Proof Reader
Carol Chapman – PA to C Wycliffe Noble

For the use of information in Chapter 2: Venue descriptions

BFI London IMAX® Cinema, London

Alex Page – Cinema Manager
Architects: Avery Associates Architects, London
                 Garry Reynolds – Associate Architect
Photography: Richard Holttum
Section drawing by Avery Associates Architects.

Brixworth Library, Northampton

I J Clarke – Principal Librarian West
Architects: Ian Shepherd, D5 Architects, Birmingham
Photography: Bob Fielding, Northamptonshire County
                 Council

Edinburgh Castle, Edinburgh

Barbara Fraser – Press and Publicity Manager
Historic Scotland, Edinburgh
Numbered drawing from Historic Scotland, Edinburgh.

Grosvenor Museum, Chester

Steve Woolfall – Museums Officer
Architects: Chester City Council,
                 Construction, Design and Management
                 Service
Photography: Simon Warburton – Museum Photographer

The Museum of Science and Industry, Manchester

R L Scott – Acting Director
Architects: Austin-Smith: Lord
Photography: Jean Horsfall

The Museum of Worcester Porcelain, Worcester

Amanda Savidge – Museum Manager
Architects: Stainburn, Taylor Architects, Ledbury
                 Stephen Taylor
Photography: Paul Higham – for Stainburn Taylor
                 (building photographs)
                 Dennis Stone (interior displays)
Numbered plan from Stainburn Taylor Architects.

National Railway Museum, York

Hilary Selvin – Display/Project Administrator
Photography: National Railway Museum

Papworth Everard Library, Cambridge

Mrs Leonore Charlton – Development and Marketing Manager
Architects: Frank Shaw Associates Ltd, Cambridge
                 Paul Phelps
Photography: Libraries and Information, Cambridgeshire
                 County Council

Royal Academy of Dramatic Art, London

Nicholas Barter, Royal Academy of Dramatic Art
Architects: Avery Associates Architects, London
                 Garry Reynolds, Associate Architect
Photography: Mark Tupper
                 Richard Bryant, The Factory, Kingston upon
                 Thames, Surrey.
Section drawing and floor plans by Avery Associates
Architects.

Royal Albert Hall, London

Ian Blackburn – Director of Building Development
Architects: Building Design Partnership, London
                 Martin Ward – Architect
Photography: Royal Albert Hall
                 Sally Ann Norman, Sally Ann Norman
                 Photography, Newcastle on Tyne
Plans and section drawing by Building Design Partnership.

Royal Shakespeare Company, Stratford upon Avon

Dean Asker – Communications Officer – Royal Shakespeare
Theatre, Stratford
Architects: Michael Reardon (for the Swan Theatre)
Photography: Zharar Chaudry – Royal Shakespeare
                 Company Photographer
                 Simon McBride
Seating plans from the Royal Shakespeare Company.

Somerset House Trust, London

Diana Hansen – Director – Somerset House Trust
Architects: Peter Inskip and Peter Jenkins, London
                 Peter Jenkins
                 Donald Insall Associates, London
                 Tony Dyson
                 Jeremy Dixon, Edward Jones, London
                 Michael Trigg

Photography: Aerial photograph by
Realistic Photo Graphics Ltd, Wallington,
Surrey
Fountains at Night photograph by
Peter Durant via ArcBlue On Line Picture
Library, Richmond, Surrey
Numbered diagram of Somerset House from Somerset House
Trust.
Drawings from Jeremy Dixon, Edward Jones.

Current conservation advisers: Fielden and Mawson
Alan Robson

For the use of information in Chapter 3: Examples of good practice

Royal National Theatre, London

Ros Hayes – Senior House Manager
Architects: Sir Denys Lasdun

National Portrait Gallery, London

Lucy Ribeiro – Access Officer
Architects: Jeremy Dixon, Edward Jones, London
Balcony Gallery
Photography: Kim Noble

Lloyd's Building, London. Ramp

Architect: Lord Richard Rogers

Thorne House, Claygate, Surrey

Architects: C Wycliffe Noble and Associates
Photography: Sam Lambert

Cité des Sciences Musée, Paris

Photography: Michael Lamoureux

Cartoons

Architect, Cartoonist, Illustrator   Louis Hellman MBE, London

Handrails

IR Security and Safety Ltd – Laidlaw, Willenhall, West Midlands

Pathways

Resin Bonded Gravel
Sure Set UK Ltd – Specialist Surfacing Contractors, Warminster, Wiltshire

Contributors who have also assisted in the preparation of this publication

Stewart Coulter, Director   The ADAPT Trust
Peter Monk   Reader – Communication Techniques
Marcus Weisen, Arts Officer   Royal National Institute for the Deaf (RNID)

Publisher

Alison Yates – Commissioning Editor
Liz Whiting – Editorial Assistant   Elsevier Limited

Photography – others

Photography was also undertaken by the joint authors and by

Jan Noble BA (Hons)
Kim Noble BA (Hons)

1 Development of the Journey Sequence

This concept was developed to replace what had become a fragmented method of assessment used when identifying barriers in buildings and providing solutions.

Isolated situations of access surfaced and often a priority for dealing with a solution was taken out of context from what should have been a comprehensive review of the various elements that made up a satisfactory environment.

At the request of the European Commission, a European conference organised by the Dutch Council of the Disabled was held in Utrecht in October 1987 on 'Access to public buildings for the handicapped'. The aim was to generate new initiatives to improve access to the built environment in the European Community. One of the recommendations of the conference was that the main general access measures should be harmonised and standardised within Europe. The Utrecht conference developed this recommendation further by advising the European Commission to compile a European Manual. The Central Coordinating Commission for the Promotion of Accessibility (CCPT) consequently took the initiative for the development of this manual, financed by the European Commission and supervised by a steering group of experts from different European countries.

The steering group accepted the practice set down by member C Wycliffe Noble, that elements in a building should not be looked at in an isolated manner but a formula for an assessment of a building should be based on a journey sequence.

In other words when identifying a provision up to and within a building, the journey from commencement to conclusion should be used to validate what was required.

A review of isolated parts of a building, which disregarded a comprehensive sequence of mobility within it, would inevitably lead to an unsatisfactory design solution.

Thus emerged the method that has been termed 'The Journey Sequence'.

Eventually the European Manual was replaced in November 1995, by 'The European Concept for Access', which sets down dimensional criteria as a basis for European Harmonization of Accessibility standards and guidelines.

The Journey Sequence formula of assessment is now incorporated into that document and it is accepted in many other documents, at European and International level, as the basis for validating the built environment.

The principles to identify elements in the Journey Sequence are as follows:

THE JOURNEY SEQUENCE[1]

- Place to Park
- Place to be Set Down
- Approach to the Building
- The Building Entrance
- Lateral Circulation
- Vertical Circulation – Stairs and Lifts
- Reception and Box Office
- Auditoria
- Backstage Facilities
- Rehearsal Rooms

[1]Copyright Mr C Wycliffe Noble OBE.

- Performer Dressing Rooms and Facilities
- Bars and Restaurants
- Bookshop
- Offices
- Conference/Meeting Rooms
- Unisex WCs
- Staff Rooms
- Technical Aids
- Communication System for the Hearing Impaired
- Systems for the Visually Impaired
- Signage

For certain purpose groups of buildings, further zones of use can be incorporated into the sequence.

It is used in this book to identify the various elements of the built environment.

Designing for people with disabilities

1.0	PEOPLE WITH SIGHT IMPAIRMENTS
1.1	Lighting – natural and artificial
1.2	Absence of shadows
1.3	Size of letters on signs
1.4	Raised letters on signs
1.5	Braille on signs
1.6	Tactile information on stair handrails
1.7	Tactile information on corridor handrails
1.8	Tactile information on doors
1.9	Tactile information on floor surface
1.10	Tactile information at perimeters for directional use – colour contrast texture
1.11	Acoustic information and wayfinding cues
1.12	Aromal information – planting
1.13	Uncluttered circulation areas
1.14	Floor surfaces and wall decoration – to reduce visual confusion

2 Venue descriptions

Royal Albert Hall, Kensington Gore, London

Restoring the Hall for future generations

Since opening in 1871, the Royal Albert Hall, sited off Kensington Gore, London, has occupied a central position in the cultural life of the nation. Each year more than a million people attend a wide variety of events including, of course, the world's most prestigious music festival the – BBC Proms.

The first comprehensive programme of development since the Hall's construction aims for completion in 2003, costing a little over £70 million and is supported by grants from Heritage Lottery Fund and the Arts Council. The programme will transform this historic building to meet the needs of the people of the twenty-first century.

The architectural masterplan has at its heart a simple idea – the removal and concentration of all services to an underground basement and access point under the South Steps. This has liberated considerable space, rationalising and improving all the Hall's facilities, enabling the interior to be restored and improving the approaches to the building. The new service yard increases the efficiency of the Hall and protects its neighbours from the nuisance of service traffic.

The public circulation areas have been refurbished and the bars and restaurants in the Circle are complete; new generous bars have been provided for the Arena and Stalls audiences. The number of public lavatories has been increased and all existing facilities upgraded. The auditorium has benefited most of all: it has been substantially reseated, air conditioning installed, the great organ refurbished and furnishings and colours selected to complete the transformation.

The external environment of the Royal Albert Hall has, over a period, become obscured by parked vehicles, through traffic, the clutter of road markings, street furniture and a variety of different materials. A radical reassessment of that situation leads to new solutions which will enhance the genius loci of the Hall.

Parking

Designated parking spaces, with a call point, for disabled drivers and passengers are situated on the north side of the Hall leading to accessible entrances.

The removal of staff car parking to underground accommodation will provide increased supervised space for parking for disabled drivers and passengers.

Other parking spaces for VIPs can be allocated by arrangement in the underground service yard with access ramps linking dressing rooms and level access to stage.

Approach to the building

A uniform surface will unite the wider precinct around the Hall, harmonising with the York stone. The surface will be comfortable for wheelchair users, pedestrians, and robust enough for permitted traffic.

Accessible entrances

Stepped access points are provided with handrails.

The South Steps project has freed space inside the building to improve amenities for the public, production staff and performers. Now completed, all delivery traffic has access to the Hall underground service yard, thus reducing disruption to the residents and visitors.

The area under the South Steps has been excavated to allow for the construction of new basement levels housing plant rooms, new accessible dressing rooms and an underground loading bay.

The Memorial to the 1851 Exhibition has been restored, the steps replaced, and the gardens relandscaped. The steps lead up to a new South Porch, which will house a box office, access to a new shop and a remodelled restaurant. This provides daytime visitors with a magnificent approach to the refurbished hall.

Reception and box offices

The box office is now located in the south foyer, to be accessed via the new South Porch ramped entrance from Prince Consort Road.

The box office and layout have been designed so a member of staff who uses a wheelchair, as well as a disabled visitor, is provided with facilities based on ergonomic principles for the design and levels of ticket desks. Induction loops have been installed.

Stairs – lifts

All main staircase steps are fitted with nosings in colour contrast to treads.

In addition to Victorian-style cast iron guardrails, smaller rails for the benefit of ambulant people are installed.

New lifts are installed with voice-over announcements, and lift buttons, contrasted and embossed, are illuminated and supplemented with Braille signals.

Stalls

There have been many achievements, not least the complete reseating of the Stalls. This involved the removal of old timber floors and beams and their replacement with new structural steelwork and pre-finished decking, new seats and Arena stairs. The new structure provides safer and more comfortable access for disabled people. Rails at the end of seat rows are provided.

Loggia and Grand Tier Boxes

Loggia and Grand Tier Boxes and corridors were newly refurbished for the Proms in 2001. Work is scheduled to repair the Gallery, and the roof has been reglazed and repaired.

The Choir seating area has also been completely refurbished with new and more comfortable seats.

Circle

The Circle structure has been rebuilt with new improved upholstered seating. Wheelchair designated spaces are provided in Circle P R W Y opposite staircases east and west, of which P and Y have better sightlines. These provide positions parallel to the Circle front to allow uninterrupted sightlines.

Gallery

This level is principally a technical area for lighting major productions but may be used by a standing audience for some events and for receptions. There is lift access for wheelchair users to this level.

Dressing rooms

Existing dressing rooms have been refurbished with level or ramped access to the rear of the stage. Principal rooms have en-suite toilet facilities.

Unisex toilets are located in proximity to other dressing rooms.

The dressing rooms, previously occupying a large amount of space in the sub-basement, have been relocated to the accommodation under the South Steps. Accommodation is therefore provided for choirs, orchestras and bands, some members of whom may be disabled.

Performers' access to stage

The two routes of the Bull Run provide access points from the dressing rooms to the back of the stage.

This provides part of a comprehensive plan to ensure that disabled actors and performers have a convenient and barrier-free route to participate in a variety of productions.

Disabled technical and management staff involved in setting up productions and maintaining the building are located in accessible offices and workshops in the new basement levels. These areas are linked by ramps and lifts. Toilets are available on all levels.

Restaurants and bars

The sub-Arena areas have been transformed into two large foyers.

The Prince Consort Wine Bar and Café at Grand Tier level and the Victoria Room Brasserie at Circle level have a flexible layout allowing accessible seating for disabled people.

The Elgar Room Restaurant is situated at Circle level. The upper and lower level is connected by a stairway and a short rise accessible platform lift for the use of disabled patrons.

Bars have accessible shelving and two-tier pedestal tables at accessible levels.

In the Boxes, for the convenience of patrons, refreshments can be provided by prior arrangement.

Toilets

Unisex toilets for disabled people are accessible from the corridors and lobbies surrounding the Hall.

In addition to those for performers and staff, unisex toilets for patrons are located at:

Ground Floor level
Grand Tier level
Circle level

Communication systems for hearing and visually impaired people

All audiences now enjoy greater comfort without audible noise from the ventilation system, which is important for people with hearing impairments. A new infra-red sound system has been installed.

Audio description will be made from a specially insulated broadcasting booth.

A comprehensive signage system has been developed for easy way-finding.

Guides

A new access guide is being prepared to provide advance information for people with disabilities.

ROYAL ALBERT HALL

1. 'The Hall's vision for providing improved access in a heritage setting'.

Since opening in 1871 the Royal Albert Hall, sited off Kensington Gore, London, occupies a central position in the cultural life of the nation.

2. The external environment has been the subject of a radical reassessment leading to new solutions.

2

2

2

2

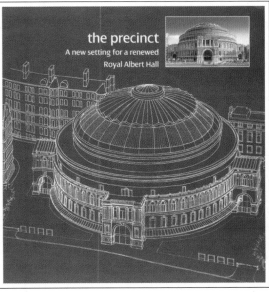

the precinct
A new setting for a renewed
Royal Albert Hall

1

Colour plate 1

Royal Albert Hall

1. Designated parking spaces for disabled drivers and passengers.
2. Vehicle call point providing assistance for access to car park.
3. Designated access points lead to perimeter paving protected by a continuous canopy.
4. An infra–red system has been installed for people with hearing impairments.
5. The Circle has been rebuilt and provides spaces for wheelchair users and companions.
6. New seating has been provided in the Stalls with space in the Grand Tier Box area for wheelchair users and companions.
7. A comprehensive signage system has been developed for easy way-finding.

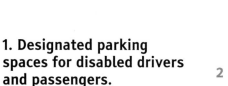

Royal Albert Hall

1. Blended kerb access points from car park to perimeter paving.
2. Stepped access points are provided with support handrails.
3. Temporary access ramp and steps with slip resistant surfaces.
4. South Porch new ramp with stone details matched to the existing architectural quality.

Royal Albert Hall

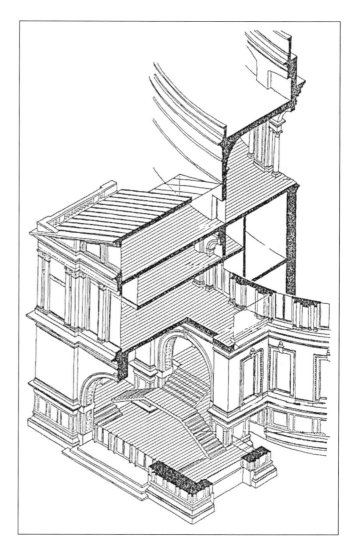

1

1. New South Porch accessible main entrance.
2. The ticket office, located in the South Porch foyer, is designed to enable both staff and visitors who are disabled, to use the desk and facilities. Induction loops are provided.

2

Royal Albert Hall

1

2

3

1. All main staircases are fitted with nosings in colour contrast to the treads.
2. Victorian–style iron guardrails are supplemented with small hand grip rails for ambulant people.
3. New lifts are installed with voiceover announcements. Lift buttons, contrasted and embossed, are illuminated. These are supplemented with Braille signs.
4. The stepped Stalls are provided with support rails at the entry to each row of seats.

4

4

Royal Albert Hall

1

1

1. Stepped and
ramped access from
dressing rooms to
stage ensure
performers have a
barrier–free route in
order to participate
in a variety of
performances.
2. Dressing room
layouts are
adjustable and are
adjacent to unisex
toilets and shower
facilities.
3. The Elgar Room
Restaurant is on two
levels connected by
a stairway and short
rise lift.

2

3   3

Royal Albert Hall

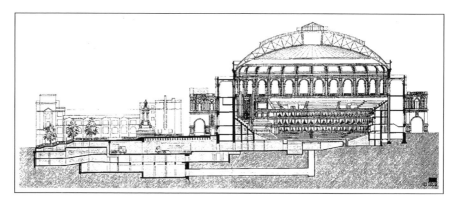

Cross–section showing the new basement areas providing vehicle parking and loading bay to rear of stage, workshops and new dressing rooms.

Royal Albert Hall plans

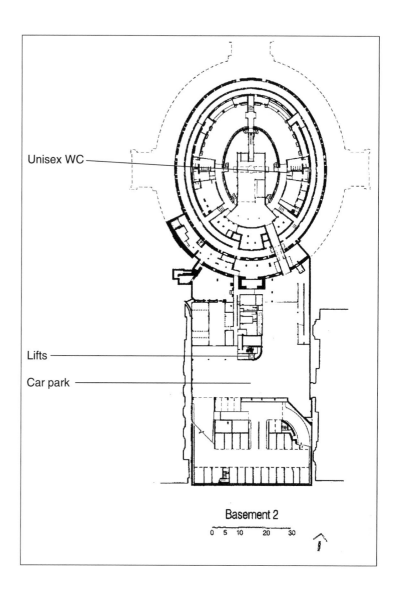

Unisex WC

Lifts

Car park

Basement 2

0 5 10   20   30

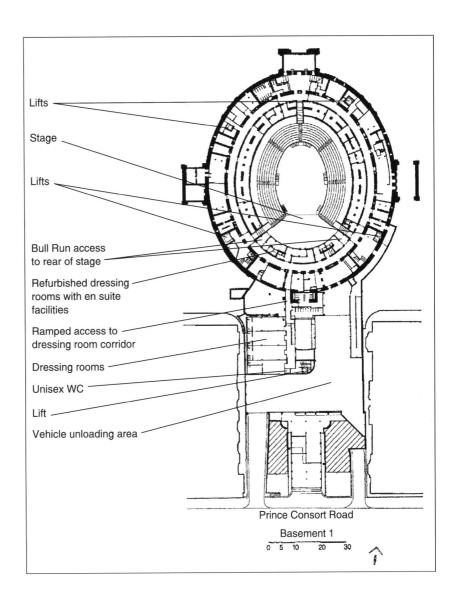

Lifts

Stage

Lifts

Bull Run access
to rear of stage

Refurbished dressing
rooms with en suite
facilities

Ramped access to
dressing room corridor

Dressing rooms

Unisex WC

Lift

Vehicle unloading area

Prince Consort Road

Basement 1

0   5   10   20   30

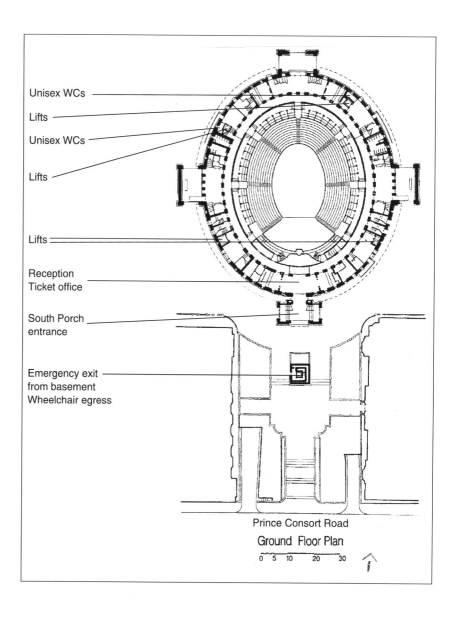

Unisex WCs

Lifts

Unisex WCs

Lifts

Lifts

Reception
Ticket office

South Porch
entrance

Emergency exit
from basement
Wheelchair egress

Prince Consort Road

Ground Floor Plan

0   5   10   20   30

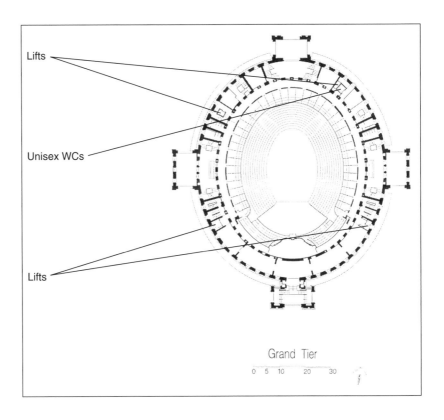

Lifts

Unisex WCs

Lifts

Grand Tier

0 5 10   20   30

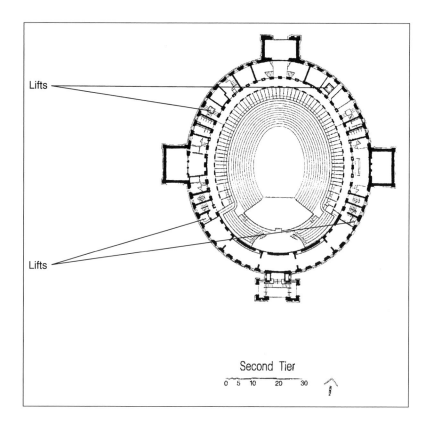

Lifts

Lifts

Second Tier

0 5 10   20   30

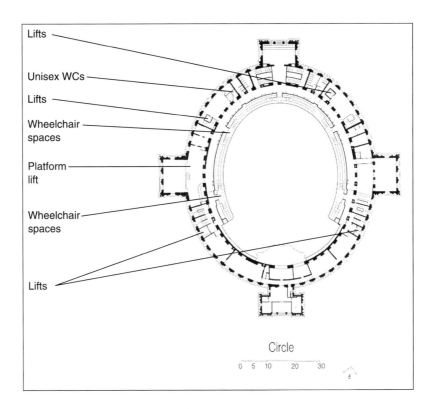

Lifts

Unisex WCs

Lifts

Wheelchair
spaces

Platform
lift

Wheelchair
spaces

Lifts

Circle

0   5   10   20   30

The Royal Shakespeare Company, Stratford upon Avon

The Royal Shakespeare Company in Stratford upon Avon has two theatres sited in proximity to each other on the banks of the River Avon.

The Royal Shakespeare Theatre, the main structure, is a Grade II listed building built in 1932 and the older of the two, the other theatre being the Swan. Proposals to upgrade the theatres and supporting facilities with a Lottery funded grant are in development.

The Royal Shakespeare Theatre

The theatre, due to its age, has problems of access principally related to the auditorium design, particularly as there is no lift to the circle and balcony, and to the lack of adequate and comfortable circulation areas and features to cater for an audience of 1400, some of whom will be elderly or disabled.

Parking and approach to the building

However, there are many provisions made for people with disabilities. There is ramped access from car park to foyer. Level access is existent in the foyer and routes to the stalls with designated spaces for disabled patrons. An accessible unisex WC is situated near the foyer.

Restaurant

'1564', the river terrace restaurant and bar, is a feature enjoyed by patrons in a riverside venue, and has level access from the theatre's foyer.

Swan Theatre

Approach to the building

The approach to the building is via a gently sloping ramp 1:20 with central handrail. Entrance to the building is via steps or alternatively via a ramp. Access to the auditorium is via a ramp or steps and there are designated spaces for wheelchair users.

The foyer has two fully accessible toilets.

Horizontal circulation

This theatre, with excellent sightlines from seating provision from the surrounding areas and galleries, brings the audience in close relationship with actors for productions in the round.

Facilities for hearing impaired patrons

Sign interpreted performances

Sign interpreted performances in BSL are available in the Royal Shakespeare Theatre. A sign-language user should inform the box office when booking for these performances, so that the patron can be allocated a seat with a clear view of the signer.

Captioned performances

Captioned performances are available in the Royal Shakespeare Theatre and the Swan. The captioning box is positioned in different locations for different shows so the box office will make arrangements for the patron to sit where they can read the captions.

Induction loop amplification system

There are induction loop amplification systems in parts of the stalls and circle in the Royal Shakespeare Theatre and the Swan Theatre.

Infra-red

Both theatres are fitted with an infra-red system. Headsets are in the foyers of each venue and are available for use with the system, which gives hearing enhanced facilities.

Facilities for visually impaired patrons

Audio described performances are a regular part of the repertoire in both theatres and headsets are available in the theatre foyers.

A pre-show described introduction to the shows is provided before 'curtain up'. These notes are also available on cassette to listen to before you come to the theatre.

Guide dogs and hearing dogs

Dogs can be taken into the Royal Shakespeare Theatre and the Swan Theatre. Before taking the dog into the auditorium, appropriate seats can be booked. Alternatively, the dog can be left with a member of staff during the performance.

The Royal Shakespeare Theatre

1. The main entrance to the Royal Shakespeare Theatre is wide and level and accessible from the car park.
2. The foyer showing access to a unisex toilet with support rails and switches in contrast colour to wall surfaces.
3. The river terrace access door to restaurant and bar, identified with the International Symbol of Access.

The Royal Shakespeare Theatre

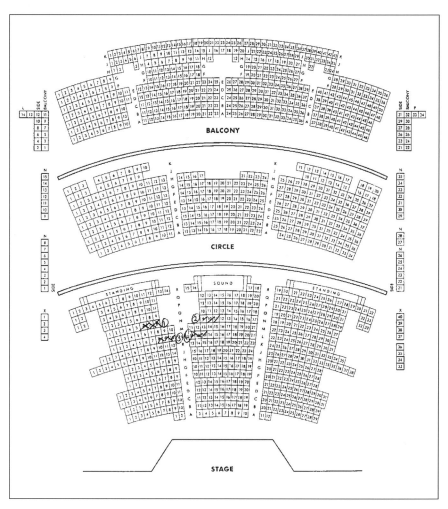

Auditorium showing allocated spaces for wheelchair users and companions.

The Swan Theatre

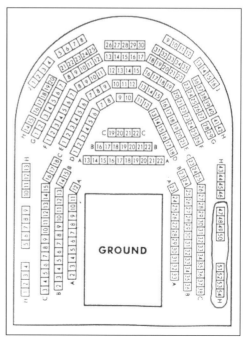

1. Building entrance with ramp and stepped access with nosings to treads in colour contrast.
2. The auditorium, with excellent sightlines from seating areas for wheelchair users, in close relationship to actors, for productions in the round.
3. Wheelchair users and companions spaces in Row H.

The Museum of Worcester Porcelain, Severn Street, Worcester

The outstanding collection of Worcester Porcelain is housed in one of the world's leading specialist museums, the Dyson Perrins Museum in Worcester. It is independent and its sole purpose is to illustrate the history of porcelain manufacture in Worcester from 1751 to the present day.

It is located three miles from the M5 junction 7, in the centre of Worcester, near to the cathedral.

The museum, which provides a design journey through time, exhibits rare porcelain, displayed in period interior settings.

The company's history is portrayed in the Georgian, Victorian and Twentieth Century Galleries, where refurbished displays include shop fronts, room settings and dining scenes.

Parking

Parking is available on site for visitors, and designated bays for disabled drivers and passengers are adjacent to the building entrance.

The bays are clearly identified by signage and the International Symbol of Access.

Approach to the building

The approach from designated parking bays is level and formed with flat granite set paving. The pedestrian routes are protected from vehicular traffic by bollards.

Accessible entrances

The entrance with double leaf doors, opening manually, has a level threshold with adequate circulation space outside and inside, accessible for ambulant and wheelchair users.

1. The Royal Shakespeare Theatre, Stratford, sited on the banks of the Avon, is a Grade II listed building constructed in 1932.
2. The river terrace is accessible from the restaurant and bar.
3. Approach to the theatre is via a gently sloping ramp gradient 1:20. The central handrail provides support for ambulant people when ascending or descending.
4. Slip resistant paved surfaces provide safe access for wheelchair users.

Colour plate 3

1

2

Museum of Worcester Porcelain

3

1. The approach, from designated parking bays, is level, formed with flat granite set paving and protected from vehicular traffic by bollards.

2. The accessible entrance has a level threshold with adequate circulation space, outside and inside, with seating for use by disabled people.

3. At accessible, ground floor level, room settings have a high quality of display illumination.

4. Access to first floor level is by lift and short rise lift. The staircase is fitted with step nosing in contrasting colour and handrails of a profile which are easy to grip.

4

Horizontal circulation

The existent two-storey building is Victorian, housing the porcelain collection.

From the reception area there is a level route through to the display areas.

At ground floor level the displays and the room settings have high quality illumination and the cabinets each have a vignette with good legible captioning, which sets the scene for a period and identifies the exhibits.

Individual exhibits are placed at levels which can be viewed by young people and those who are wheelchair users.

There is access by lift to the upper storey.

A short rise platform lift provides an accessible route between the two upper levels.

The staircase is fitted with step nosings in contrasting colour and handrails are of a profile that is easy to grip.

The new single-storey Exhibition Hall was opened in the autumn of 1999.

Restaurant

The Warmstry Restaurant adjacent to the museum is open seven days a week in elegant surroundings where you can enjoy morning coffee, lunch and afternoon tea.

Shops

The factory shop, situated as you come in the main entrance, sells first and second quality fine bone china, porcelain, tableware, giftware and clearance lines at factory prices.

Toilets

An accessible unisex toilet is situated at ground floor level with the entrance via the Georgian Gallery Service display area.

Communication systems for the hearing and visually impaired

Large-scale print-outs of information are available to assist those with sensory impairments.

Trained tour guides are available to assist disabled people.

A taped tour of the gallery is planned.

The Museum of Worcester Porcelain

1. New extension. Level entrance and east elevation.
2. Display cabinets incorporate a vignette with legible captioning which sets the scene for the period, at a height viewable by young people and wheelchair users.

The Museum of Worcester Porcelain

Plans showing location of access, lifts and toilets.

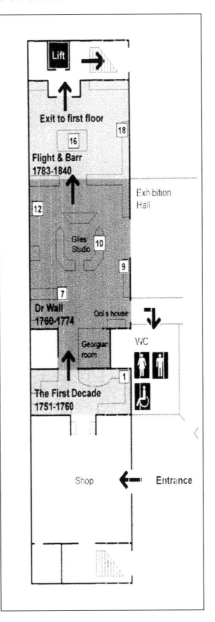

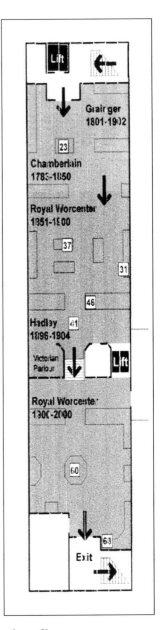

Ground floor

Case No:

1. Wigornia Creamboat
7. Scale Blue
9. Blind Earl Pattern
10. Exotic Birds
12. Gloucester Service
16. Royal Lilly and The Royal Warrant
18. Prince Regent Service

First floor

Case No:

23. Nelson Teapot
31. Aesthetic Teapot
37. Worcester Enamels
41. Chicago Vase
46. Owen Vase
60. American Birds
68. Painted Fruit

Somerset House, Courtyard, South Building and River Terrace, The Strand, London

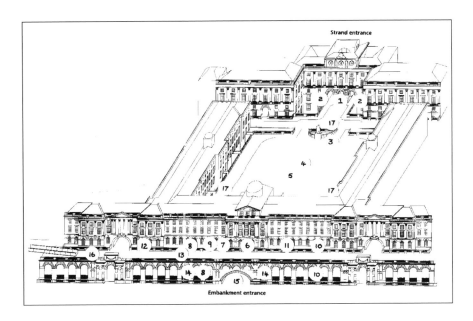

1. Strand Entrance
2. Courtauld Institute Gallery, Café and Shop
3. George III statue
4. Edmond J Safra Fountain Court
5. Courtyard
6. Seamen's Waiting Hall
7. The Admiralty Restaurant. Bar and Deli
8. Lavatories and baby changing facilities
9. Navy Office Entrance
10. Stamp Stair
11. Hermitage Rooms and Shop
12. Nelson Stair
13. River Terrace and Summer Café
14. Gilbert Collection Galleries and Shop, Embankment
15. Great Arch, Somerset House Introductory Gallery, King's Barge House and The Old Palace Exhibition
16. Access to Waterloo Bridge
17. Lightwells (no public access except on guided tour)

SOMERSET HOUSE

1. Somerset House, the eighteenth century classic masterpiece of Sir William Chambers, occupying a prominent position on the north bank of the River Thames, extending north to the Strand.
2. Accessible, level and stepped entrance from the Strand.
3. The pedestrian link from Waterloo Bridge provides access to the River Terrace and Summer Café.
4. Entering the accessible Courtyard from the Strand one is aware of the huge scale of the building.

SOMERSET HOUSE

5

5

6

7

5. The approach to the Embankment entrance, South Building, is via a ramp and short rise lift.
6. Entrance to the South Building is via the curved ramps.
7. Sloping crossovers cut into the granite kerbs between pavement and carriageway.
8. The Seamen's Hall is the centre of the horizontal east–west circulation connecting the Nelson Staircase, cloakrooms, lifts and restaurants.
9. Clear signage is located at strategic way-finding locations.

9

8

Somerset House, the eighteenth century classical master-piece of architect Sir William Chambers, occupies a prominent position on the north bank of the River Thames extending back as far as the Strand.

The original building projected into the river but was separated in 1870 by the construction of the present Embankment carriageway.

Entering the Courtyard from the Strand, one is aware of the huge scale of the building, enclosing three sides of the quadrangle by five-storey façades, two storeys of which, below Courtyard level, are hidden behind a surrounding stone balustrade. The Piranesian areas thus produced are spectacularly bridged to form entrances to the surrounding buildings just above Courtyard level. Chambers cleverly exploited the change in level across the site to increase the amount of accommodation.

Phased development

While members of the public had been able to visit the Courtauld Institute Galleries, set in the refurbished Strand Block of Somerset House since 1989, most of Sir William Chambers' magnificent building, including the Courtyard and its surrounding buildings, remained a part of hidden London largely closed off to the general public and used as Civil Service offices.

In 1997, following departure of the Civil Servants, except Inland Revenue staff, the Government set up the Somerset House Trust with the aim of making the building once more available to the public and to re-establish it in its setting.

The first phase of work for the Heather Trust for the Arts was the refurbishment of the Embankment Building and parts of the South Building as galleries for the Gilbert Collection of Decorative Arts.

The second phase of the works consisted of the refurbishment of the Courtyard, the public areas in the

South Building and the River Terrace, all being connected by a major new pedestrian route from the Strand to Waterloo Bridge.

The Courtyard, the River Terrace and the pedestrian link to Waterloo Bridge are the principal external environmental features reviewed here, the chronology being as follows:

1990	Courtauld Galleries established
1996	Inskip and Jenkins report on reuse of the building; they were commissioned for £33m phase 1 – including the Gilbert Collection.
1997	Somerset House Trust established
1998	Construction of Phase 1 commenced
	Donald Insall Associates appointed as Lead Architects for £15m Phase 2, with Dixon Jones appointed to design the River Terrace café structure and pedestrian link to Waterloo Bridge
1999	Appointment of C Wycliffe Noble as Disability Planning Adviser
1999	Construction of Phase 2 commenced
2000	Gilbert Collection, Courtyard and River Terrace open to the public
	Courtyard fountains inaugurated (designed by Dixon Jones, Donald Insall Associates and Light Matters)
	Hermitage Rooms open
	Possible later phases include moving the Courtauld Galleries to the upper floors of the South Building, accessed via the Nelson stair and lifts

Parking

Except for servicing the building, access to the Courtyard is for pedestrians only, with a limited area of public parking for disabled drivers and passengers nearby. Near to the Strand and Embankment entrances designated parking bays in adjacent streets are available and there is limited parking during the evening on one side of Waterloo Bridge.

Approach to the building

There are controlled pedestrian crossings to the Strand entrance from Arundel Street, Wellington Street, Melbourne Place and the Strand. Wheelchair access is provided from the Strand pavement, through the central archway, along the carriageway.

The approach to the Embankment entrance South Building is via a ramp and to other levels via a short rise lift, passenger lifts and stairs.

Sloping crossovers cut into the granite kerbs between pavement and carriageway provide access for wheelchair users entering the Courtauld Institute and Courtauld Galleries either side of the carriageway. The access route from the upper terrace down to Courtyard level is surfaced with existing old granite sets, which for historical and technical reasons, cannot be removed. From the upper terrace perimeter pavements, steps which have been newly fitted with handrails also lead down to Courtyard level.

The earlier tarmac surface of the Courtyard has been replaced with lightly textured Portuguese granite sets. Access for the ambulant disabled and wheelchair users from the granite York stone perimeter paving of the Courtyard is by ramped crossovers in the kerbs.

The South Building main entrance

The outer entrances to the ground floor level of the South Building from the Courtyard are accessed by curved ramps discretely bridging the areas below. Way-finding illumination is provided in the ramp surface. An internal lift then connects this level to the Embankment entrance.

Horizontal circulation

On the ground floor the Seamen's Hall is at the centre of the horizontal east–west circulation connecting the Nelson Staircase, cloakrooms, lifts and restaurant, to the Hermitage

Rooms, crossing the north–south axis from the Strand to the River Terrace.

The Link Bridge

The new pedestrian route from the Strand to Waterloo Bridge passes along the River Terrace via the new Link Bridge, which consists of a gentle sloping ramp of 1:21, with a slip resistant surface, the bold guardrail concealing way-finding lighting on the underside.

The River Terrace

On the River Terrace the café seating areas are on raised timber platforms with ramped and stepped access and the umbrella canopies and glass sides provide a protected area from the pedestrian through-routes along the Terrace. At the east end there is access for disabled people to the ground floor of the South Building. The possibility of access for people with disabilities directly into the Seamen's Hall is under review in the longer term.

The Courtyard

The refurbishment of the Courtyard has included the provision of a high degree of servicing for major events. For the enjoyment of patrons with hearing impairments, a loop induction system is provided in the Courtyard.

An exciting feature is an array of fountainheads that projects 55 individual jets of water from the central section of the Courtyard, each finger of water being brilliantly illuminated at night by fibre optic lighting.

The kerbs of the perimeter pavements have been discretely punctuated with access points for removable crowd control barriers and electrical supply boxes, which rise from the surface for use at major events.

The War Memorial, designed by Edwin Lutyens, originally set in the middle of the Courtyard, has been re-erected on the River Terrace. Taking advantage of Chambers' Piranesian-like areas around the perimeter of the Courtyard, a large services building has been inserted at mid-basement level, running below the south end of the Courtyard. The building contains lavatories to cater for an event audience of 3500, extensive services and plant for the fountains.

The performance area of the Courtyard for outside events is backed by facilities for artists and performers. Rooms in the South Building are changed easily into dressing rooms with accessible toilets and access leading via ramps to performer spaces in the round.

During events there are toilets for disabled people on the ground floor of the South Building accessible via ramps from the Courtyard or by lifts inside the building.

In the winter an ice skating rink provides enjoyment for skaters and spectators.

Clear signage is located at strategic way-finding locations.

Somerset House

1. The Courtyard tarmac surfaces have been replaced with lightly textured Portuguese granite sets with ramped crossovers to the perimeter paving.
2. From the upper terrace perimeter pavements, steps fitted with handrails also lead down to Courtyard level.
3. An array of fountainheads that projects 55 individual jets of water from the central section of the Courtyard, each finger of water being brilliantly illuminated at night by fibre optic lighting.

Somerset House

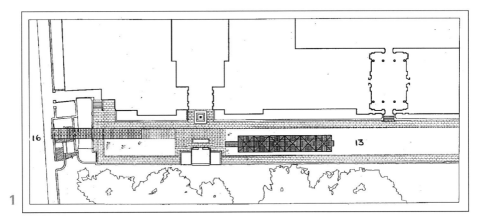

13. River Terrace and Summer Café
16. Access to Waterloo Bridge

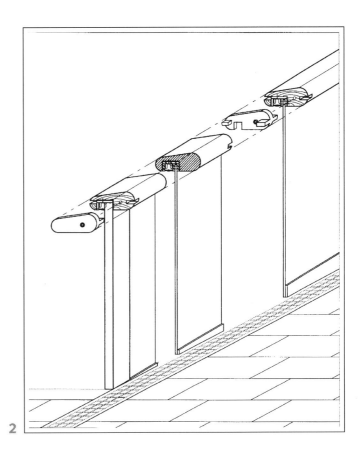

1. Plan of location of link bridge and Terrace Café.
2. Link bridge guardrail incorporating way–finding lighting.

Somerset House

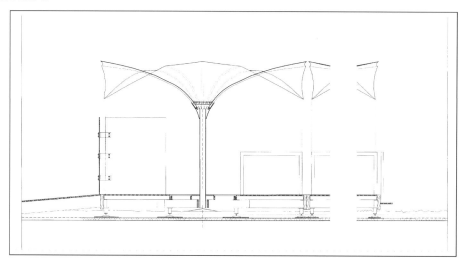

1

1. The Summer Café is on raised timber platforms with ramped and stepped access. The umbrella canopies and glass sides provide a protected area from the pedestrian routes on the terrace.

1

BFI London IMAX® Cinema, 1 Charlie Chaplin Walk, South Bank, Waterloo, London

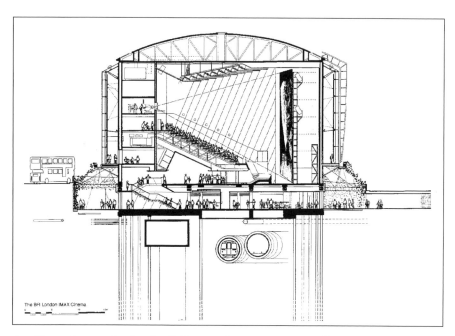

The BFI London IMAX Cinema

Section through the building. The 750 mm walls are a barrier to external traffic noise and the high standard of insulation creates a quiet ambience of benefit to people with hearing impairments.

A new landmark for London is the British Film Institute IMAX® Cinema.

The glass-enclosed cylinder is seven storeys high, a prominent focus at the south end of Waterloo Bridge.

The building is set within a vehicle roundabout and incorporates dampers so it is immune from vibration from the network of busy tunnels directly beneath it.

The 750 mm walls are a barrier to external traffic noise. The high standard of insulation creates a quiet ambience of benefit to those with hearing impairments.

Viewed from the outside, within the glass-enclosing envelope, is a giant mural by Howard Hodgkin, one of Britain's distinguished artists.

Approach to the building

The BFI London IMAX® Cinema is located in close proximity to Waterloo main line station and Underground station and is reached by use of pedestrian subways.

Vehicle access and parking

Access for vehicles by arrangement with the cinema management is via Belvedere Road to a private, secure access lane. This will allow a disabled person to disembark in the area adjacent to the entrance concourse.

Cars can be parked in the adjacent NCP car park off Belvedere Road.

Accessible entrance

The entrance to the cinema from the lower concourse level, below street level, is via ramps from Waterloo Bridge and the station. The main entrance doors open automatically. The inner foyer area provides level access to the reception area, lift lobby, main staircase, café and accessible toilets.

Reception

The ticket desk, with four ticket desk monitors, incorporates a lower-level section for the convenience of disabled persons.

Vertical circulation

Lifts and the main staircase provide access to the stepped auditorium and the first floor lobby.

The first floor lobby and ground floor foyer can be used as areas for receptions, displays and exhibitions.

Auditorium

The stepped auditorium is accessible from the lifts and spaces for wheelchair users and companions are provided with level access. At the entrance to each seating row, on the aisles, is a handrail providing assistance for the ambulant user, an important feature for stepped auditoria.

The screen is the largest in the UK, the height of five double decker buses, 26 metres high and 20 metres wide.

It has a digital sound system with the power of 11600 watts and the advanced 2D/3D projection system creates a living experience where the patron becomes part of that reality.

Restaurants

The café on the ground floor has a flexible seating arrangement with pedestal type tables usable by people in wheelchairs.

Toilets

There are accessible toilets on the ground floor via the foyer and on all other floors.

Communication systems

The cinema has been designed for use by everyone with lift access and provision for disabled patrons. Audio description of the screening of films for the blind and partially sighted is available. A loop induction system for those with hearing impairment is installed.

There are foreign language translations available for overseas visitors.

BFI London IMAX® Cinema

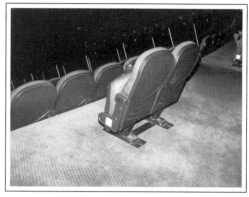

1. A support rail at the entrance to seating rows in the stepped auditorium is an important facility to ambulant people.
2. The stepped auditorium is accessible by lifts. Spaces for wheelchair users and companions are provided with level circulation areas.
3. The café provides flexible seating arrangements with pedestal type tables.
4. Accessible unisex toilets.
5. Accessible low–level telephone.

BFI London IMAX® Cinema

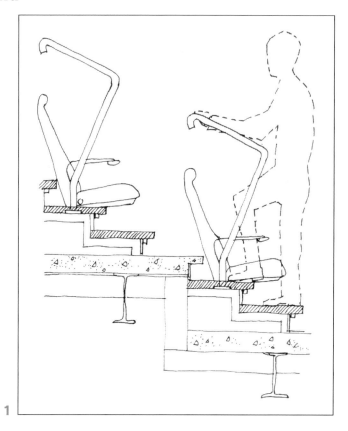

1. A support rail at the entrance to seating rows in the stepped auditorium is an important facility to ambulant people.
2. Stepped auditorium.

BFI London IMAX® Cinema

1. A prominent focus at the south end of Waterloo Bridge is the British Film Industry London IMAX® Cinema, a glass-enclosed cylinder seven storeys high.
2. The foyer area provides level access to lift lobby, café and accessible toilets. Access to upper floor levels is by lift or staircase.
3. The approach to the building, below the vehicular roundabout, is by a series of underground subways.
4. The staircase incorporates step nosings in contrasting colour with a handrail that extends beyond the bottom and top of each flight.
5. Reception foyer area with ticket monitors and lower desk section for the convenience of disabled patrons.

1

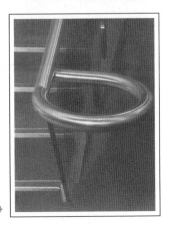

2

3

4

5

1

ROYAL ACADAMY OF DRAMATIC ART

2

3

1. Principal entrance –
Malet Street.
2. Malet Street public
entrance protected by
canopy with gently sloping
approach.
3. Entrance foyer with lower
reception counter.
4. The Jerwood Vanbrugh
Theatre on three accessible
levels providing seating for
200 people.

4

Colour plate 8

The Royal Academy of Dramatic Art, 62–64 Gower Street, London WC1E 6ED

Introduction

RADA's dream of a modern fully equipped academy on the site that had been their home for almost a hundred years became a reality when an Arts Council of England lottery grant of £22.7m was secured in 1996. Construction work began in July 1997, but before completion in October 2000 a further £8m had to be raised in matching partnership funding to enable the academy to complete what was known as the Centenary Project. Central to the Centenary Project was the new building in Gower/Malet Street, which cost £17m.

The expansion of RADA and its courses had been considerable since the early 1980s and in 1990 an annexe building was acquired in nearby Chenies Street. A comprehensive master plan was developed for both sites and gradually a new library, refectory, prop workshop and additional rehearsal rooms were created in the converted Chenies Street building. On the main site at Gower/Malet Street the task was to provide new wood and metal workshops, a scenery assembly area, which was to include a paintframe, further teaching and rehearsal rooms, a wardrobe department, sound studios, administrative offices, three fully equipped performance spaces to public entertainment licence standard, and a foyer/bar that by day was to be a student area and by night the public bar/foyer to all three performance spaces.

In many respects, the location and orientation of the principal performance space was the crucial factor in resolving the public/private circulation pattern. This space, the Jerwood Vanbrugh Theatre, was to be a multi-functional/flexible proscenium arch theatre with a capacity of 200.

Approach to the building

The entrance from Malet Street has been made the principal public (performance) entrance and that from Gower Street the principal private (academy) entrance, each having its own quite different character.

Vertical and horizontal circulation

The Academy's desire to retain many of the original features of the Gower Street building, notably the GBS theatre, ground floor reception and main stairwell, proved a considerable challenge for the design team. With the assistance of disabled access consultants a strategy for upgrading these areas of historical importance and integrating them within the new scheme was developed to ensure good access for people with disabilities. The structure in the Gower Street building was substantially modified to enlarge the existing lift shaft and provide routes through to the Malet Street building. The complex changes of level inherited from the Gower Street building, which is at a different level from Malet Street, also made it necessary to include a small number of platform lifts. All three auditoria are fully accessible both to stage and audience side, including even the high-level tension wire lighting grid in the Vanbrugh auditorium where sufficient space has been allowed to give access to wheelchair users.

The Jerwood Vanbrugh Theatre

Undoubtedly the greatest challenge of the project was to compress the full range of facilities that a modern drama school like RADA required into such a very constrained urban site and nowhere is this more apparent than in the design of the principal auditorium – the Jerwood Vanbrugh Theatre.

Over 200 seats have been fitted on three levels with stalls and two balconies.

The Jerwood Vanbrugh Theatre is truly a multi-purpose accessible space, used for teaching, rehearsals and social events, as well as for performances. It therefore has a glass wall at the rear to bring daylight in from a 'cleft' light well, a seven-piece hydraulically operated elevating floor and a unique system of double, multiple-hinged proscenium flaps on each side of the stage. The flaps can be adjusted in combination with the elevating floor sections to create a multiplicity of configurations of proscenium arches, Juliet balconies, orchestra pits and/or forestage areas etc. plus promenade, courtyard and 'in the round' settings.

The Royal Academy of Dramatic Art

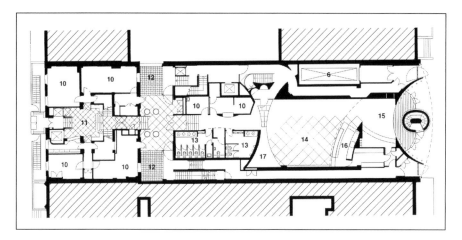

  6. Goods Lift
10. Offices
11. Gower Street Reception
12. External Light Well
13. Public WCs
14. Malet Street Foyer
15. Box Office
16. Bar
17. Cleft Light Well

Plan showing Gower Street and Malet Street ground floor entrances.

The Royal Academy of Dramatic Art

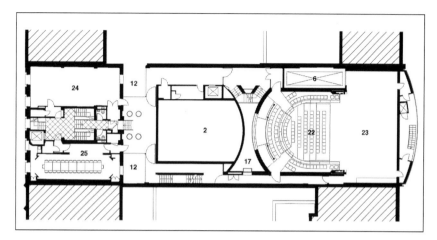

2. Void
6. Goods Lift
12. External Light Well
17. Cleft Light Well
22. Jerwood Vanbrugh
23. Stage
24. Acting Room
25. Council Meeting Room

The Jerwood Vanbrugh Theatre is a multi-purpose accessible space used for teaching, rehearsal, performances and social events.

The Royal Academy of Dramatic Art

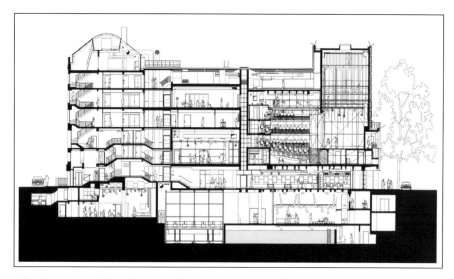

The Jerwood Vanbrugh Theatre is a multi–purpose accessible space used for teaching, rehearsal, performances and social events.

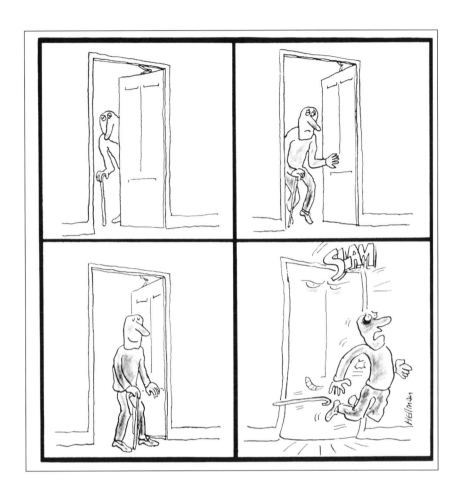

Edinburgh Castle, Edinburgh, Scotland

'Built to keep people out: now encouraging them in'

Edinburgh Castle dominates the skyline of Scotland's capital city and is a world-renowned symbol of everything Scottish. As the fortress grew through the centuries it was far more adept at keeping people out than welcoming them in.

Times change and Edinburgh Castle is now Scotland's premier visitor attraction. More than 1.2 million people a year approach its drawbridge and make their way up the steep climb to reach Crown Square, home of the 'Honours of Scotland', the Great Hall and the National War Memorial.

Historic Scotland, the government agency that cares for Edinburgh Castle, is very aware that as many people as possible should have effective access to so many potent national symbols. Consequently it has put in place a number of solutions.

Approach to the building

A courtesy vehicle, sponsored by the Bank of Scotland, is in daily use and is fitted with a hydraulic lifting system that makes transporting visitors and their wheelchairs as easy as possible. It can carry two wheelchairs and six passengers at any one time, and picks up visitors from the castle esplanade and delivers them to Crown Square, the highest part of the Castle. The vehicle is operated by a core of 12 of the Castle's stewards, who volunteered to be trained in using the car and helping people with disabilities.

Accessible entrance and vertical circulation

The 'Honours of Scotland', crown, sword and sceptre, are the oldest regalia in the United Kingdom and among the oldest surviving in Christendom. Just outside today's Crown Room is a hands-on model of the Honours and a Braille interpretation of their history. A new entrance has been provided for those visitors whose mobility is impaired. There is a lift up to the Crown room and ramped access for most wheelchair users. The National War Museum of Scotland offers free entry to visitors and is accessible throughout to wheelchair users.

Horizontal circulation

The National War Memorial is also entered from Crown Square. A ramp for access is now completed and was designed to make as little impact as possible on the exterior façade of the Memorial designed by famous Scottish architect Sir Robert Lorimer. The simple but unobtrusive design is a good example of a sensitive adaptation that does not detract from the architectural significance of the building and greatly improves accessibility, especially for the high number of disabled ex-servicemen and women who visit the Memorial. The new stone ramp was hand-carved by masons from Historic Scotland's Monument Conservation Unit and cost around £3000.

Communication systems

Exploring the Castle is made easier for people with visual impairment through provision of an audio tour and Braille guides, free to visually impaired people. The audio tour is the longest such tour of any attraction in the UK and provides a wealth of information.

It is only to be expected that in such a historic venue there will be difficulties with access. There are cobbled surfaces, and in some entrance areas sensitive treatment has ensured that steps have been replaced by level stone materials.

The modifications undertaken at Edinburgh Castle over a number of years underline the sensitivity of meeting the needs of visitors but also preserving the built heritage for future generations.

Edinburgh Castle numbered drawing.

1. Esplanade
2. Palace Block
3. Great Hall
4. Crown Square
5. War Memorial
6. National War Museum
7. Café

Papworth Everard Library, Papworth Everard, Cambridge

'Cooperation to stimulate excellence'

This stimulating centre of excellence built in 2000 and funded from the Sir Jules Thorn Trust is a joint venture between Cambridgeshire Libraries, the Varrier-Jones Foundation and the Papworth Trust. It provides a community library for everyone living and working in the village of Papworth Everard. The architects and design team consulted with clients and staff at every stage of the project. This has resulted in the careful integration of a wide range of special features and technology to aid access, in a beautiful, elegant library. It is developing as a 'teaching library', providing training in all aspects of library work for clients of the Papworth Trust. There are three part-time library staff and 11 volunteers from the Papworth Trust, all of whom have a disability. The library is part of the redevelopment of a former light industrial site that employed patients from the former Papworth Tuberculosis Settlement. The building is the first in a larger development that will include shops and a café in a prime location in the centre of the village. The mature trees that border the site have been retained, softening and providing shelter for the new building which is clearly visible from the main road. The building is managed by the Varrier-Jones Foundation and also houses the Disabled Living Centre, the Disability Information Service and the Housing Design Service.

Car parking and public transport

The car parks have been designed to provide ample parking space for those both visiting and working in the building. The main car park includes two designated spaces adjacent to the library building and two designated spaces for minibuses transporting people with disabilities. The side car park has six designated spaces for those with disabilities. Additional space has been provided next to these allocated bays to enable easy access to vehicles. Dropped kerbs and tactile paving have been installed at appropriate points in both car parks. There is a drop-off point at the front of the main building providing level access to the footpath that surrounds the whole of the building. The bus stop is situated on the main road 25 metres from the main door and is accessible via a gentle gradient.

Approach to the building

Visitors approach the building either by ramp from the main road, linking to the level footpath, or by the footpath from the car parks. The ramp also provides access to the first floor and there is also an external lift accessible from the car parks.

Building entrances

The main entrance doors are glass, outward opening, automatic doors designed with a timing device for people using wheelchairs.

The reception counter for all organisations in the building is located just inside the doors. The main door and all other entrance doors comprise glass with etched circles. All the entrances on the ground floor open directly onto the level footpath.

The library stretches the complete length of the building on the left side and there is open access from the foyer into the library. Consequently, parents with double buggies and wheelchair users are able to move easily into the library. The library has a 'feature' garden. Doors have level access to the sensory garden, outside event space and drama studio, giving the potential for linked artistic and literary events.

The double glass doors with etched circles are the main fire exit from the library.

A separate door for staff is situated at the rear and is suitable for wheelchair users. An electronic swiped key system is used to make access easy for staff and clients with disabilities while still maintaining the security of the building.

Library reception/information point

The low-level counter area with an island worktop allows space for knees and wheelchairs both sides of the reception desk. On the counter there is a large button telephone and a hands-free bar code scanner, as well as two computers for the library issue system.

The wide, open and uncluttered library design gives plenty of room for wheelchair and buggy manoeuvring, and there is a simple arrangement of resources. The library is divided informally into six main areas: non-fiction, fiction, browsing, relaxing area, study, and children's areas. There is a full range of adult and children's lending, study and reference facilities, also the ICT service described below, plus photocopying, fax, video and music CD loan services. 'Doorstep' volunteers use the library to deliver books to local housebound people.

Every effort made to ensure all equipment is accessible is reflected in the choice of appropriate shelving and units. The new Gresswell Xolys shelving has been used and is low level so that wheelchair users can access all levels of books, whether as readers or members of staff. This is high quality shelving with a modern design featuring inset coloured steel bars in a light wood frame, free standing and secure so it can be rearranged for either flat display or for multimedia information. The shelving was selected for its adaptability, clean, clear lines, attractive appearance and ease of adjustment, so that the units can be combined in imaginative ways. The children's area has a teardrop table and picture book browsing boxes combined with bookshelves in a streamlined arrangement.

The computer benching was designed after tests with clients to ensure the optimum height for comfortable wheelchair access. For customers with special requirements there are two height-adjustable tables worked by a simple winding mechanism. These are used at present for the CCTV and Braille machines.

The seating combines the formal and informal with a range of stylish chairs for study, computer use and comfortable reading. The colour co-ordinated chairs, with and without arms, incorporate a variety of upright, low designs and special sizes for children.

The study tables have a central pedestal leg feature to assist wheelchair users to sit comfortably without the need to negotiate table legs.

In the children's area there is an interactive, tactile feature incorporating a peacock, bees and birds. A bubble tube with light, colour and moving fish gives added sensory stimulation and interest.

It has long been recognised that good clear guiding, or signage, is required to help users find their way around libraries. The main library guiding is large, white, upper and lower case lettering on a peacock blue background. The signs are either wall mounted or suspended from the ceiling. The lettering on the shelf guides has been made as clear and large as possible.

ICT

A wide range of access technology is available for people with visual impairments, learning difficulties and limited motor skills, including:

- seven computer terminals for free public use with internet access, email, desktop publishing, library catalogue, community information and careers guidance;
- word processing packages using symbols and drawings;
- touch screen facilities, on-screen keyboard and mouse facilities;
- voice synthesisers to all software;
- adapted keyboards, guards and mice;
- text to Braille translator and printer;
- CCTV machine and text enlarger on TV screen;
- loop hearing system.

Vertical circulation

The main entrance is well signposted from the road and car parks. The shared entrance area has adapted public toilets, an internal lift and stairs to the upper floor. The external ramp, lift and stairs also provide access from the main road and car parks to office and conference facilities on the upper floor. The controls in the lifts are also in Braille and all the stair treads have suitable nosings.

Horizontal circulation

There is level access to all parts of the ground floor from both the main and library entrances, and similarly there is level access to all accommodation on the first floor. All doors are wheelchair accessible and have raised colour contrasting strips on the opening edge and along the bottom of the door. The library is carpeted throughout in a heavy-duty durable carpet suitable for wheelchair and buggy use, and safety flooring has been installed in the joint-use kitchen area on the ground floor.

Toilets

These are situated in the main foyer adjacent to the library. The toilet for users with a disability has been designed to a high specification and includes a hoist and emergency cord, with colour contrast for floor, walls and tiles. Large signs are used on the doors to indicate which is for male, female or adapted use: this toilet measures $0.7\,\text{m} \times 2.15\,\text{m}$, and has a large handle for easy access.

Office

The office-cum-workroom is fully accessible and used daily by trainees and staff, while many of the administrative routines take place in the main area of the library.

Systems for visually impaired people

The colour scheme was chosen to link with the Papworth tapestry displayed outside the library. When the tapestry was created peacocks roamed the grounds of the elegant Papworth Hall, now home to the Trust that still retains the parkland setting. A peacock in the tapestry provided the inspiration for the vibrant colours used in the library with effective colour contrasts for people with visual impairments. The walls have been painted a lemon colour to contrast with the blues and greens in the carpeting, shelving, furniture and signage.

Large windows have been incorporated into the design of the library to provide plenty of natural light and ventilation. Ceiling spotlights are used to supplement the natural light on dark days and in the evenings.

Guide dogs are welcomed into the library in line with the policy for all libraries in Cambridgeshire.

The stock of books reflects special emphasis on a wide selection of spoken word cassettes and large print books, and the children's library has Big Books for loan or use in the library, and Braille/text picture books from the 'Clearvision' loan service. All leaflets are obtainable on cassette and in Braille; a large print version of the library guide and an audio guide are available.

Systems for hearing impaired people

There is a hearing induction loop within the counter reception area and in other parts of the building.

Fire exits

The garden door in the library is the main fire exit and leads onto the level footpath. The staff entrance at the rear of the library is also a fire exit and leads out into the main foyer. The exits are clearly signed. The doors in the library are fail-safe opening doors and they unlock automatically in the event of a fire or the activation of a fire alarm, and the library shutter closes automatically in the event of fire.

Publicity

The colourful library leaflet 'A place for everyone' is available in large print and as an audio cassette or in Braille. There have been two open days, and a friends group has started to support events and fundraising for specific projects. Due to the unique nature of the library it has received wide publicity especially throughout the library and information profession.

Training

A training programme has been designed to give clients with disabilities the opportunity to develop their skills and to work alongside staff who then gain the experience of working in partnership. Workshops, awareness sessions, and local and national seminars ensure the dissemination of best practice.

The £208 000 library is the first of its kind in the United Kingdom, managed by Cambridgeshire County Council as a public library with training for disabled people, and its success is in bringing together all parts of the community as a cornerstone of the redevelopment of the village centre.

The National Railway Museum, York

'All aboard: access for all'

The National Railway Museum opened in York in September 1975. The buildings it now occupies once belonged to British Rail and are redolent of the railway history it preserves and portrays, but turning them into a modern national museum has presented a unique and interesting array of challenges. Not only must it maintain high standards for its visiting public (which earned it the Yorkshire Tourist Board White Rose Award for Tourism 2001, European Museum of the Year 2001 and the Dibner Award for Excellence in Museum Exhibits 2002), but also take into account the needs of disabled staff members to whom it has a duty.

The Museum's personal commitment to improving access is enshrined in two of its core objectives, i.e. first, 'to communicate with the widest public in inspiring, enlightening and enjoyable ways' and second, 'to continuously improve the quality of the service we offer'.

In order to give this philosophy a corporeal form, the NRM sensibly allied itself to existing speciality groups and guidelines.

It is a member of the Employers Forum on Disability and ensures that it follows its ten points for access for action in every area of its work. It also follows the access policy created by the National Museum of Science and Industry of which it is a part and has established an internal Advisory Group on Access (AGA), a corps of staff members that meets every quarter. Each member of the group brings a special knowledge of access issues which enables the Museum to regularly keep abreast of internal matters, legal requirements, the provision of services to and communication with disabled people, available sponsorship, education and training opportunities for staff and the forging of new links with speciality groups.

EDINBURGH CASTLE

1. Edinburgh Castle dominates the skyline of the capital city of Scotland. It is a world renowned symbol and the premier visitor attraction.
2. National War Museum new canopied entrance lobby for those visitors whose mobility is impaired. Lifts and ramps provide access for wheelchair users.
3. Ramped access to the National War Memorial is designed with materials and details in keeping with the architectural heritage of the surrounding areas.

1

2

3

PAPWORTH EVERARD LIBRARY, CAMBRIDGE

1. Visitors approach the building by ramp or by lift from the car park. The ramp also provides access to the first floor.
2. The library includes a feature garden. The sensory garden has space for outside events and drama giving the potential for linked artistic and literary presentations.
3. Shelving, which is at lower level, is accessible to wheelchair users, whether as readers or members of staff.

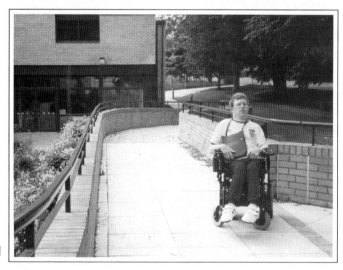

1

2

3

NATIONAL RAILWAY MUSEUM, YORK

1. The National Railway Museum opened in York in September 1975. The buildings, reminiscent of railway history, provide a unique array of displays.
2. The miniature railway provides space for wheelchair users. James Fisher waves the green flag to start the journey.
3. A full size, accessible carriage of the Series 0 'bullet train' from the West Japan Railway Company is accessed by a range of ramps.

MUSEUM OF SCIENCE AND INDUSTRY, MANCHESTER

1. and 3. The five buildings comprising the museum are linked together with smooth external pathways and ramps.
2. The museum displays and hands-on exhibits are accessible to people with impaired vision or learning difficulties as well as to young children and older people.

Making links with these outside groups has helped with initiatives such as the production for an access leaflet that follows the Royal National Institute for the Blind's 'See It Right' clear print guidelines. The leaflet provides general information about the NRM to people with special needs and their carers. The same guidelines are used in the interpretative labels that accompany the Museum's exhibits. It is hoped that a similar, equally fruitful, relationship can be cultivated with the Royal National Institute for Deaf People.

Staff and volunteers who deal with the public are enrolled on the Yorkshire Tourist Board's 'Welcome All' training and most of the Explainers have completed the Visual Impairment Awareness Training course run by the Blind and Partially Sighted Society.

Physical access to the Museum begins before the visitor ever comes within sight of its walls.

Approach to the building
The Road Train provides a seasonal shuttle service to and from York city centre and can carry two wheelchair users at a time.

Accessible entrance
Since there are two public entrances, parking has been designated for the city entrance, which allows level access to the Museum.

Horizontal circulation
The NRM consists of three main exhibition areas: the Great Hall, the Station Hall and The Works. As all three halls also house staff in either an administrative or technical capacity, the NRM has had to create an environment that is suitable for both the visiting public and employees and volunteers who may require special access.

The entire 17-acre site has been adapted to accommodate wheelchair users. Old track flange recesses in the Great Hall floor have been in-filled to provide level passage, and all the essential services and facilities, such as admission prices, the restaurant, toilets, lifts and telephones have been created with attention to special needs.

The National Railway Museum was offered a Series O 'bullet train' pantograph car, built in 1976, from JR West (West Japan Railway Company). It was accepted into the NRM's collection because it is such an important object in modern railway history. The Japanese train was adapted to provide access to and within the train, which is viewable by all visitors.

Emergency egress procedures are crafted to ensure that disabled people can be evacuated safely and efficiently. There is also provision for disabled staff who can access their places of work via the ramp at the staff and goods entrance.

Communication systems

The NRM's dedication to ensuring that the widest possible audience can enjoy its collections is demonstrated by the enduring success of its annual 'Please Touch' evening. Once a year visitors with special needs are invited to the Museum free of charge after usual opening hours to explore the exhibits by touch, sound and smell. Although the Museum has an ideological commitment to the continuing improvement of its services to the community, in practice this is limited by the budgetary constraints of being a nationally funded organisation.

The Advisory Group on Access helps to identify sources of funding, which most recently resulted in Taylor Woodrow's sponsorship of a groundbreaking new miniature railway carriage, designed to transport wheelchair users, and is believed to be unique. For the first time, the popular miniature railway at the NRM can be enjoyed by an entirely new sector of the public.

Toilets

A grant from the ADAPT Trust and the conferring of one of its main Millennial Awards for good practice has meant that the Museum has been able to outfit its newest wing, 'The Works', with up-to-date toilet and baby changing facilities, and an automatic door opener leading to the balcony overlooking York railway station. This makes it easier for those in wheelchairs and those pushing prams or pushchairs to see the famous views over the station.

Vertical circulation

Elsewhere in the same development an open-topped, glass-sided lift was incorporated to ensure equity of access and a view across the Museum's Great Hall.

The work of constantly improving access to the National Railway Museum never ends. The NRM actively encourages feedback from its visitors to ensure that its facilities and services match their needs.

It has introduced a Customer Services Initiative Form, available to all visitors, undertakes four exit surveys a year and participates in an annual York-wide visitor survey. By placing itself under this constant public scrutiny and by subscribing to so many key policies and access schemes, it has ensured that it will always keep itself true to the philosophy it expresses in its mission statement and keep track of the issues faced by all museums in the twenty-first century.

The National Railway Museum

1. Station Hall ramp.
2. Accessible wagon ramp.
3. Shinkansen Train accessible carriage door.

The Museum of Science and Industry, Manchester

'Creating the joined-up museum'

In 1994 the Museum of Science and Industry in Manchester was given the British Gas Special Award by ADAPT as the cultural organisation that had done most over the previous three years to improve its premises and services for people with disabilities.

The museum, set on a seven acre site, is on two levels, 6 metres apart.

There are five buildings:

- Main Building
- 1830 Warehouse
- Station Building
- Power Hall
- Air and Space Hall

They are linked together with a network of smooth pathways, ramps and lifts.

In 1996 work commenced on a scheme that would complete the Museum, making it one of the largest of its kind in the world, with excellent facilities for all visitors. A generous grant awarded by the Heritage Lottery Fund and support by the European Union and Department of Culture, Media and Sport enabled detailed design work to begin. The concepts that underlie 'The Final Phase' are inspired by the Museum's mission statement:

> The Museum of Science and Industry in Manchester will use its remarkable site, the world's oldest railway station, and its collections to create a museum of international standing which has as its overall theme the industrial city, thereby capitalising on Manchester's unique past, contributing towards its future prosperity and fostering the pleasure of understanding for a broad public.

There is a potential conflict between two objectives expressed by the mission statement. The 'remarkable site' comprises five large listed historic buildings (two of which are Grade 1), structures such as bridges and viaducts, and external spaces including yards and railway tracks.

The 'broad public' includes all sections of society, including people with restricted mobility, impaired vision or learning difficulties as well as young children and the elderly. The strategy seeks to balance the need to protect the historic fabric of the site with the commitment to make the entire Museum as accessible as possible. In particular, the Museum is determined to integrate facilities and services so that people's needs are anticipated and all visitors can share the same experience, rather than requiring special arrangements.

The site has presented particular challenges. Only two of the buildings were ever intended to be open to the public.

The passenger station was inaugurated in 1830 as part of the Manchester terminus of the Liverpool and Manchester Railway.

The building that is now the Air and Space Hall opened in 1877 as the Lower Campfield Market.

The other buildings designed for the shipment of goods by rail were two warehouses and a freight shed.

Smooth slip resistant linear pathways have been incorporated into the granite set areas thus retaining the genius loci of the place, while providing comfortable and safe access to buildings. The site is bisected by a fenced railway line, on which Friends of the Museum operate steam train rides.

The network of smooth paths now links all the buildings. Its installation provided the opportunity to join up the Museum with a cabled IT network. A third ingredient of the joined-up Museum was a new orientation system to introduce visitors to the site and enable them to find their way around it. Legibility and the use of bright colours for the signs were criteria to enable people with restricted vision to navigate the Museum. A significant development was the installation of a staircase and lift tower to serve all the levels of the main building, and to provide visitors with a more direct route to the lower courtyard level. Here they discover the new Collections Centre in which the reserve collections are stored in a way that makes them visible, with managed access for those who wish to go behind the scenes.

A new entrance and shop provides a welcoming introduction to the Museum, with the emphasis placed on easy access. Materials and colours have been used to create good contrasts for people with visual impairment and recommendations from the access adviser have directed many aspects of the 3D design.

Improvements to the Museum's physical facilities have been accompanied by measures to ensure that the needs of people with disabilities are always part of the thinking of staff. Training is one aspect of this, for example in the Sympathetic Hearing Scheme and sign language interpretation.

The most powerful experience, however, was the hosting of the temporary exhibition 'Dialogue in the Dark' in which a number of everyday situations (a kitchen, bar, park, road etc.) were presented in total darkness. A team of partially sighted and blind guides was recruited to guide visitors through the exhibition, which had a profound impact on all who experienced it. This in turn has encouraged the inclusion of 'The Senses' as one of the themes of the new 'Interactives' Gallery. The power of hands-on exhibits to communicate with visitors with disabilities is something of which management and staff have become very aware. The response of visitors with learning difficulties has been particularly encouraging. This is an important group of users, including employees, as the Museum has participated in the 'Breakthrough' Scheme for many years.

The Final Phase project presented the Museum with a great opportunity to build on the good practice and experience that ADAPT had recognised in 1994 and addresses the numerous issues of access that still existed. The objective of creating the joined-up Museum was adopted as a way of making physical and conceptual links between the components of a very large complex of historic buildings, galleries, support facilities and external spaces. The objective was one of the ingredients of the brief that was prepared for the architects and the services' consultants. Detailed design was developed with a Museum team as clients. Market research with visitors was used to inform the approach to access, and an access adviser was engaged.

The fundamental indication of whether the Museum of Science and Industry in Manchester has succeeded in addressing the needs of visitors with disabilities is the response by visitors themselves.

It is heartening that every day the Museum attracts many people for whom visitor attractions are often a daunting prospect. By putting in physical facilities, by designing exhibitions to be accessible, by listening to suggestions and criticism, and by providing a friendly welcome for all, visitors can expect a trouble-free, enjoyable experience.

The Museum of Science and Industry

1

2

1. Way-finding and site signage to the five buildings is part of the orientation system introduced as part of the joined-up museum philosophy.
2. New lift and stair tower in the Main Building.
3. Smooth path and ramped entrance to the 1830 Warehouse.

3

Grosvenor Museum, Chester

'A millennium makeover for a Victorian site'

The Grosvenor Museum, in Chester city centre, was originally built in 1886. A further extension was added in 1896 and a separate Town House, dating to 1680, joined via a link corridor to the Victorian building in the 1950s. A set of offices adjacent to the Town House and a further set adjacent to the Grosvenor Street building were added in the 1950s and 1980s respectively. All four additions have different floor levels from the original 1886 building. The ground floor alone contained three changes of levels.

The ground floor access scheme

This provided an innovative and integrated solution to the challenges of providing access in a multi-level listed Victorian building. The involvement of disabled people in the development of the scheme added to its value as a case study for other such difficult community buildings.

The scheme cost approximately £535 000, with funding coming from a number of sources. The Museum followed a Journey Sequence in access, reproduced here in brief as a descriptive example.

The comprehensive approach in considering the needs of disabled people took account of the following:

Physical access: helping visitors get around the building.

Attitudinal access: providing what visitors want and making them feel welcome.

Intellectual access: helping visitors enjoy and learn from the collections.

Virtual access: 'Cataline', a computerised database with images of objects on display; video tours in the lecture theatre; photographic albums of exhibitions; other parallel work on the building, on displays and for information services.

A Journey Sequence

Car parking, place to be set down and public transport

There are two designated spaces for Orange/Blue Badge holders within 24 metres of the Grosvenor Street entrance.

There is also a designated coach drop-off facility within 25 metres of the same entrance. The pedestrian route from the main shopping centre of the city features dropped kerbs, pedestrian controlled lights at the key crossing point and 'finger post' signage on the route.

The Museum is situated on the bus routes serving the south of the city together with a stop for the Wrexham Road 'Park and Ride' service that uses accessible buses. There is a peak-time bus service to the railway station within 25 metres. There is capacity for taxi and Dial-A-Ride drop-off outside the Grosvenor Street entrance and a 'Shopmobility' scheme operates in the city centre, with an accessible route from its base to the Museum.

The Bunce Street rear entrance also provides parking for powered chairs and access to the ground floor for users via lifts.

Approach to the building

There is no change of level from the designated car parking provision or on the pedestrian route to either entrance.

Entrance to the building

The Grosvenor Street entrance was originally accessed via seven steps, and this entrance has been completely remodelled to incorporate lift access and new steps for ambulant people. The steps have tactile marking in a mosaic pattern to link with the existing historic entrance hall interior. The heavy glass entrance doors have been replaced by automatic doors.

The new entrance/exit from Bunce Street that links to the nearby historic Chester Castle area has been created with level access and automatic doors. This entrance provided the opportunity to install a larger than standard lift to accommodate scooters and to provide users with direct access to the museum ground floor displays and facilities.

Reception/information

The Grosvenor Street entrance has a low-level reception desk, immediately adjacent to the new entrance doors, from which are available maps of the building and bound sets of Braille labels for each gallery.

Bunce Street entrance has a low-level reception desk that also serves as the counter for the adjacent shop area. It also has an induction loop and is accessible on both sides, thus enabling the employment of people with mobility disabilities as Visitor Assistants.

Staff at either desk can also arrange for the wheelchair that is available for use in the building by visitors to be brought to a suitable location. At the rear of the entrance hall there is a poster board and leaflet holders providing information about exhibitions and events in Chester and nearby attractions that may be of interest to visitors.

Vertical circulation

The ground floor contained three changes of level necessitating the installation of three lifts. As an interim measure virtual access to the displays on the upper floors, which are currently physically inaccessible to some visitors, has been developed with video tours that allow Keepers to present their galleries in a way which both acts as a virtual tour for anyone who cannot visit them and adds an extra dimension to what can be seen for those who can visit. The tours are shown in the museum lecture theatre via a video projector and accessible selection panel. These video tours, together with the introductory audio-visual presentation in the Chester Timeline Gallery, are now available for sale in the Museum shop and a copy can be lent to visitors unable to access the Museum at all.

The Cataline computerised catalogue system contains information about objects in the upper floor galleries, as well as objects not on display, together with objects in temporary exhibitions of museum collections. The system is connected to the collection's documentation database and is regularly updated. For first floor temporary exhibitions that involve collections from other institutions or private individuals, photographs of the exhibits and copy labels are produced so that visitors unable to climb the stairs can get a taste of the new displays.

A new, integrated signage system, installed in all areas and manufactured by Modulex, is in a clear typeface with high differentiation in colour between text and background. The signage also includes symbols to help those who have difficulty reading. A new map of the building was also designed and installed at both entrances.

Horizontal circulation

All three lifts have automatic doors, alarm buttons (sounding through to the permanently staffed control room) and are independently usable. Power assisted opening devices have been fitted to the doors from the entrance hall to rear foyer (where the accessible toilet is located) and lecture theatre. All other doors on the public circulation route are held open during opening hours (with magnetic closers in case of fire). Where carpets have been installed they have been chosen to have a short, dense pile suitable for wheelchair use.

Toilets

A new accessible toilet was installed as all existing toilet facilities are either up or down a flight of stairs. The new toilet is immediately adjacent to the main circulation route and is available in the evening when the museum lecture theatre is used by several local societies. The room features height-adjustable toilet and washbasin, and there is a baby changing table facility that does not affect the functioning of the toilet facility. There is a hoist available for use in the toilet for those unable to independently transfer to the seat. A range of sling sizes has been purchased to suit a variety of users.

Display areas

The Chester Timeline Gallery was developed as part of the Access Scheme to give both visitors and local residents a broad overview of the historical development of the city of Chester to modern times. It uses three levels of interpretation: a computer generated animated tour of the city through time, wall mounted graphic panels and low-level display cases with objects from each era. There are also large-scale reproductions of coins from key periods in Chester used for producing 'rubbings'. The gallery acts as a link to the rest of the museum, encouraging visitors to explore the other galleries.

The scheme also included the upgrading of the lecture theatre that features tiered seating. A wide platform area was created at the rear to provide a suitable space for wheelchair users and their companions to watch the video tours or enjoy the regular programme of talks and lectures. The video tours are subtitled for visitors with hearing difficulties. The balustrade also features slots for the storage of walking aids. All other galleries created in the past decade have been designed to be accessible to wheelchair users, even though such access was difficult at the time.

The Roman Stones Gallery is a particularly successful example of this design. All these new galleries follow a three-tier interpretation policy: large introductory boards with short, clear introductions to what is on display in that area for a reading age of about 11 years; object labels with more detailed information for a reading age of about 13; and further information computer interactive or reference files. Wherever possible the opportunity has been taken to include tactile and audio elements, together with computer interactives for those visitors who prefer to get information that way.

Shop

The Museum Shop has been housed in a number of locations over the past decade, all of which were very small thus providing little room for access or effective display of stock. In order to create full independent access to the ground floor of the Museum it was necessary to demolish the 1950s link corridor and replace it with a wider structure that would accommodate a platform lift beside the existing steps. It was decided to create an L-shaped conservatory-style link that also provided room for a larger, more accessible shop. The low-level shop counter also serves as the reception point for the Bunce Street entrance. It has an induction loop and is accessible on both sides. There is a central low-level display unit for smaller items, with other goods displayed on a mixture of freestanding units and shelving. Staff assist customers wishing to view items on upper shelves.

Office/backstage facilities

These areas were not included within the remit of the Access Scheme because of the complexities of location and changing floor levels. They will be addressed in future phases of museum development.

Tactile/audio systems for visually impaired people

Over the past ten years staff have worked with the local Talking Newspaper to record features on temporary exhibitions, new galleries and local history and have also developed a programme of 'live commentaries' (visually described tours) of temporary exhibitions and introduced two 'talking' dummies to describe life as a Roman soldier and a Victorian naturalist. Within the Access Scheme there were several features designed explicitly to help visually impaired visitors:

new signage system;
large print labels (in separate folders) for all galleries that are also used by those unable to stand for long periods to read labels;

Braille labels for all galleries – to be supplemented by thermoform pictures over the next five years;
voice for 'Maid of all Work' in Victorian Kitchen display of No. 20 Castle Street;
tactile roundels incorporated into Bunce Street gates.

Communication systems for hearing impaired people

The scheme also includes provision for visitors with hearing impairments. Supplementing existing induction loops in the lecture theatre, reception and shop areas are:

subtitles to new video presentations both in the introductory gallery and lecture theatre;
Minicom for contacting the Museum.

Emergency egress

The implementation of the Access Scheme required the complete revision of the Fire Evacuation Policy that has been approved by the City Fire Officer. Under the policy front of house staff search the building and will wait with any visitors unable to exit independently. Two new public fire exit routes were also created. Given the changes in ground floor level already mentioned, evacuation chairs were also purchased to enable the safe evacuation of all areas and floors of the building.

Publicity

Consultation with users began at the outline planning stage for the Access Scheme with meetings of interested local bodies (such as the Civic Trust), museum users (e.g. Grosvenor Museum Society) and disabled people (via Chester Access Group). Of particular importance were members of the Chester Young Disabled People's Project who worked with museum staff and the architects to develop the solutions and ensure their practicality. All these groups spread word of mouth information about the scheme. Displays of photographs of the work in progress, regularly updated, were shown in an adjacent shop window and on the Museum's website. The public reopening in August 2000 was promoted by a Millennium Makeover leaflet that was distributed to all local households and visitor attractions in the region, supplemented by banners at Chester Castle (on a major road junction) and in the Town Hall Square. A feature for the Talking Newspaper was recorded and advertisements placed in regional magazines for disabled and retired people. Both the Millennium Makeover and future venue leaflets, together with the events and exhibitions leaflet 'Don't Just Sit There', feature access information and are available in large print.

Training

Prior to building work starting on the Access Scheme all staff undertook Disability Awareness Training. This was later supplemented by an update on the Disability Discrimination Act. All new staff will also undertake similar training. All front of house staff (who act as Fire Marshals) plus other key staff, have been trained in the safe use of the evacuation chairs. Chester City Council has a programme of annual performance appraisal and training needs assessments for all staff. Under this programme museum staff regularly undertake customer care training to meet the needs of specific groups.

The future

In addition to this imaginative approach to development there is planned action on:

a second handrail on main stairs;
adding to the Cataline database with links to the website;
sound systems in displays;
duplicate refreshment facility;
display with audio track;
audio tours;
more open days, signed talks, touch sessions in integrated events;
improvement to remote store to allow extension of lift services at the Museum.

Context

One of Chester City Council's aims is to make Chester an accessible city. As a consequence, considerable efforts are being made to improve all aspects of access around the city to serve both local residents and visitors. Chester City Council believes that all get a dividend from an investment in access. The Ground Floor Access Scheme has had a very positive reception from all visitors including those with disabilities. Visitor numbers are up 30% on average since the reopening in August 2000 and the number of physically disabled people using the building has also increased dramatically.

Grosvenor Museum

1. Remodelled Grosvenor Street entrance incorporating a short rise lift and steps with handrails.
2. The Bunce Street entrance is accessible for scooter users and has automatic doors.
3. An interior lift provides access to the change of level in the entrance area.
4. Tactile and audio systems of display have been developed in a series of 'live' commentaries. These are transmitted by a 'talking' soldier and Victorian naturalist dummies.

3

4

Brixworth Library, Brixworth, Northampton

'Beyond minimum requirements of Building Regulations'

The library was opened in 1999 in a new building to replace a Portakabin structure. Most of the funding was provided by the Home Foundation, a local charity. The building houses a community hall, meeting room and coffee shop, a one-stop shop, and toilets.

The building is of striking appearance while sympathetic with its surroundings. Modern access facilities, beyond the minimum requirements of the Building Regulations, were specified, and the interior layout ensures wheelchair access to all areas of the library.

There was considerable consultation with local people and the neighbouring residential home for elderly people was a major contributor.

Full public internet access has been achieved as a result of an ADAPT award. The results attempt to provide equality of access to quality services in a rural area.

Car parking and public transport

The building has eight parking spaces for public use, with two separate spaces closer to the entrance for disabled people that do not involve the crossing of kerbs. There are two public service bus stops within 50 metres of the building. A community service bus, equipped to carry wheelchair users and serving neighbouring villages, takes people directly to the entrance on one afternoon a week.

Approach to the building

Visitors approach the building by a ramp or by two steps with a handrail.

Building entrances

Automatic sliding doors give access to a foyer. A second set of automatic sliding doors leads into the library. Both sets of doors are marked with two horizontal rows of white dots.

The staff entrance is manually operated and is accessed from a footpath in front of the building.

Reception and information point

A dual height counter, 940 mm and 715 mm high, is provided with one section equipped with a hearing loop, with a sign to indicate its presence. There are two standard telephones for staff use. There are two directional signs at the counter: one for check-in and one for check-out and enquiries.

Vertical circulation

The library has a mezzanine housing a homework centre that is reached by lift and stairs. The stairs are 1170 mm wide, finished in beech with a black strip towards the front edge of each tread. There is a handrail in beech on both sides of the staircase with grey metal panels between it and the stair treads.

On the ground floor the lift is located in the foyer. The lift door is 800 mm wide and the internal dimensions are 1090 mm wide by 1380 mm deep. There is a mirror and a handrail on the rear wall of the lift. All of the control buttons have Braille and eye-readable symbols. There are eye-readable signs on the outside of the lift at both levels.

Horizontal circulation

The ground floor is level and there are no doors in the public area. Manually operated doors lead into the staff room and to a storeroom. The foyer is paved with textured slate tiles. The library floor is carpeted with carpet tiles.

The mezzanine is level. A manually operated door, operated by a swipe card for security purposes, opens into the lift lobby, and a manually operated door leads into a storeroom. The mezzanine is carpeted with carpet tiles.

Toilets

Toilets for men and women and a separate toilet for disabled people as users of the building are located off the foyer. The cubicle for the adapted toilet measures 1450 mm wide by 1720 mm deep. All of the sanitary fittings and hand/assist rails are white with three walls in light grey colour and one in turquoise. The door is dark grey, the door frame turquoise. The floor is tiled with grey, textured slate tiles, and the cubicle is equipped with hand/assist rails, mirror, emergency cord and electric hand drier.

Office

At ground floor level there is a work room/staff room for library staff, accessed by a manually operated door opposite the library counter.

Systems for visually impaired people

There is a good level of natural lighting within the building and artificial lighting is provided by glare-free, category 2 fittings.

Colour contrast is achieved by dark blue carpet throughout, with light grey shelves and fittings in the adult area, and red shelves in the children's area. Tables have grey frames and beech tops; chairs have grey frames and beech seats and backrests. Walls and skirtings are painted very light grey and window sills are white.

Signs are blue on white at the counter and in the adult area, red on white in the children's area.

The library has a hand-held magnifier for public use. Large print books, books on tape and music on CD are available for loan. There is no charge to visually impaired people for the hire of sound recordings. 'Sound Reads', Northamptonshire Libraries and Information Services postal service can be contacted at the library.

Systems for hearing impaired people

Part of the library counter is served by a hearing loop. Videos are available for hire, some of which are captioned.

Emergency egress

An audible fire alarm serves all sections of the building. There is a separate fire exit from the ground floor and an escape stair from the mezzanine.

Publicity

An attractive series of information leaflets available in 14 pt print and also in special large print format includes:

The Housebound Readers Service;
Writ Large – new large print books;
Out Loud – new books on tape;
Your Library Service for Sheltered Housing, Residential and Day Care Centres;
Services for Blind and Partially Sighted People;
Sound Reads – talking library by post.

Publicity incorporates information on concessions for disabled people, which include: no charges for a person using the Housebound Readers Service or the Special Access Mobile Service; no charges for sound recordings and reservations for people unable to read standard N12 print with spectacles or for people with learning difficulties.

A member aged 60 or over, or a disabled person of any age, can borrow sound recordings at concessionary rates.

Training

Staff receive training in disability awareness, especially in the following: visual impairment in partnership with the Northamptonshire Association for the Blind; hearing impairment in partnership with Northampton's Centre for Deaf People.

Brixworth Library

1. Designated parking area and approach to the building is via blended kerbs to the pavement, a ramp and steps with handrails.
2. Dual height counter equipped with loop induction system.

3 Examples of good practice

The twelve buildings so far illustrated incorporate a comprehensive range of provision but beyond these there is a variety of other building types where solutions of good practice are found, in one particular design detail, worthy of exposure.

This section identifies, with captions, a selection of these and they are placed within the order of 'The Journey Sequence'.

Palace of Westminster – Commentary by Baroness Nicholson of Winterbourne

I have worked in the Palace of Westminster from 1987 when I was first a Member of Parliament in the House of Commons and since 1997 in the Upper House. To provide modern facilities and better access in such a historic and important building is not a simple matter, but serious efforts have been made in recent years especially to improve the conditions for all members and visitors, and especially those disabled people who are employed in the precincts. The access is not ideal, and it will not be possible to gain effective access to all parts, but adaptations have been made to allow working members and visitors to participate without hindrance.

We are making progress, and the input of Architect Wycliffe Noble as adviser has been significant. In 1995 the Parliamentary Works Directorate commissioned Mr Noble to prepare a report on access in both Houses. Brief details of some positive solutions are provided below as a guide.

It is right that the Mother of Parliaments should set an example in this way, and I will check that we continue to make progress.

As the first Chairman of ADAPT I witnessed a massive change in practical improvements and in attitudes at various arts and heritage venues, large and small. Whereas in 1988 there was much resistance to change, there is now less, except that with the introduction of the Disability Discrimination Act there is a tendency on the part of some owners to do the minimum that is necessary within the law, rather than being more imaginative and setting higher standards of access.

Work on sensible improvements in Building Regulations, in which the authors have been involved, will continue but it is essential that agencies such as ADAPT continue to give guidance and exert influence for improvement. I have no doubt that the influence and constructive attitude of the ADAPT Trustees and staff have contributed to improvements, and long may this continue.

Recommendations for access

One hundred and nine zones were identified in the Palace of Westminster where assessment was necessary and solutions recommended. Four of the zones where there has been implementation of the solution are:

Zone 28: Royal Court, access to the Cholmondeley Room and River Terrace–

'The access ramp from the parking area to the entrance door was too steep and not wide enough to accommodate disabled people passing in opposite directions. A temporary ramp inside the entrance was too steep. The toilet facilities were inaccessible'.

A permanent stone ramp was installed parallel to the building frontage, with a gradient of 1:15 and designed in keeping with the architecture. A new unisex toilet was formed with its separate access direct from the corridor.

Zone 22: Access to River Terrace Dining Rooms from Star Chamber Court–

'Wheelchair access was via the main vehicle crossing between the Commons Inner Court and the Commons Court. Steps, kerbs and a steep, dangerous metal ramp were in place'.

The solution was to raise the carriageway thus providing a level route by eliminating the kerbs and steps. The stepped entrance was removed and a permanent ramp was cut into the existing floor area, providing a safe route through this area.

Zone 13: Entrance to the Speaker's private residence–

'Disabled visitors are received by the Speaker in the Residence with entry from the Speaker's Court. There is a lift for access within the premises but the external steps precluded entry'.

A permanent stone ramp was installed parallel to the building frontage allowing ease of access.

Communication aids

Hearing and reading equipment has been available for some years where such a facility is needed by members.

There was no area within the Palace grounds to exercise assistance dogs. A safe, accessible area from the Cloister has been allocated.

Royal National Theatre, South Bank, London, SE1 9PX

The Royal National Theatre, set on the South Bank of the Thames, comprises three auditoriums, the Olivier, Cottesloe and Lyttelton Theatres, function rooms and restaurants, and was first opened in 1976. It was designed by architect Sir Denys Lasdun.

Since that time a programme of phased refurbishment has taken place to meet the varying needs of disabled patrons.

This has included improved facilities of vertical and horizontal access by the installation of staircase platform lifts between mezzanines and all main floor levels and the provision of ramps.

To enable people with sensory impairments to fully enjoy the performance experiences audio described performances and sign language interpreted performances with synopses are available for most performances.

An infra-red audio system is available and induction loop installations are usable in all bars, buffets, bookstalls, box offices and the main information desk.

Guide dogs can be taken into the theatre and hearing dogs for the deaf will be looked after by members of staff.

Royal National Theatre

1

2

1. Shallow ramp to the Cottesloe Theatre.
2. Glass lift tower and its sensitive modelling.
3. Lift control buttons lowered into the carefully modelled escutcheon plate.

3

3

Royal National Theatre

1. The key operated platform stair lift between mezzanine and main floors.
2. The continuous rolled handrail detail used as a cue for people with visual impairments.
3. The backstage performers' facilities of WC and shower.

1. Park House, Sandringham
Setting down point adjacent to main entrance.
Approach road raised to the building entrance level with entrance canopy protecting visitors transferring from their vehicles.
2. Somerset House, London
Blended kerbs in tooled granite between Courtyard and pavement follow the design detailing of the historic building.
3. Somerset House, London
Ramped Embankment entrance.
4. National Portrait Gallery, London
Ramp design compatible with the quality of the existing building.

Examples of Good Practice

1. Sainsbury's, Blackhall, Craigleith Road, Edinburgh. Clear identification of designated parking places.

2. National Portrait Gallery, London. Level entrance to gallery.

3. Palace of Westminster, London. Combined steps and ramp to riverside terrace.

4. Park House, Sandringham. Smooth pathways on linear routes between gravel and granite sets areas.

5. Littlehampton Station. Clear identification of entrance doors using colour contrast for architraves, door handles and visibility warning cues.

6. British Library, London. Bold identification of doors using primary colour contrast.

7. Littlehampton Station. Cantilevered ticket office counter allows unimpeded access to station staff.

1

2

3

4

5

6

7

Colour plate 11

EXAMPLES OF GOOD PRACTICE

8. National Portrait Gallery, London
Contrast of skirting, wall and floor surfaces to assist people with orientation difficulties.

9. The Museum of Scotland, Chambers Street, Edinburgh.
Circular staircase with disc identification on treads and continuous handrail on both sides of steps.

10. The Potteries Museum and Art Gallery, Stoke on Trent
Central handrail to assist those with hemiplegia when ascending and descending stairs.

11. Peninsula sited toilet with oblique and lateral transfer space either side of the WC.

12. Queen Alexandra Hospital, Hydro Therapy Unit, Worthing
Unisex toilet with colour contrast support rails. Hot water pipes recessed or protected from contact with lower limbs. Water temperature must not exceed 42°C.

13. Cité des Sciences Musée, Paris
Boy using Braille. Caption for exhibits in Braille in a museum where hands-on experiences are featured.

14. Museum of Science and Industry, Manchester
Way-finding is an essential aid for the location of routes up to and inside a building.

15. Hamburg Central Station, Germany
For people with visual or hearing impairments tactile and colour contrast cues are supplemented by audible transmitted passenger location information.

 8
 9

 10
 11
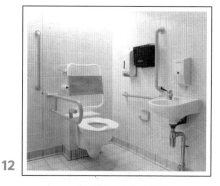 12
 13
 14 15

Colour plate 12

1

1. Scottish
National Gallery
of Modern Art,
Belford Road,
Edinburgh
An unobtrusive
ramp set in a
landscaped
forecourt.
2. RIBA HQ,
London
Combined ramp
and steps
compatible with
external façade
design.
3. Palace of
Westminster,
London
Ramp with stone
detailing,
compatible with a
Victorian heritage
building.
4. Thorne House,
Claygate, Surrey
Inclined wide
paved forecourt
under cover of
building.

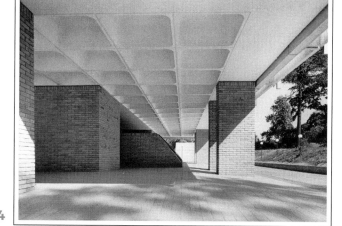

2

3

4

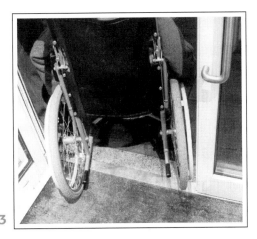

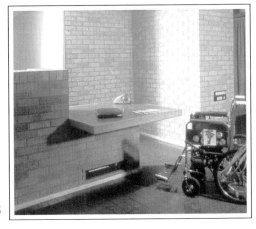

1. Resin bonded aggregate provides a textured, firm and smooth surface.
2. Walled Garden, Sunbury, Middlesex
Rolled Breedon gravel on hardcore provides a firm surface of a quality suitable for historical gardens.
3. The Joseph Rowntree Foundation, Caledonia House, London
Entrance door width allowing clearance for hands on wheelchair rims.
4. National Portrait Gallery, London
Reception desk with lowered section for visitors and staff.
5. Prospect Hall, Birmingham
Reception desk with lower section for disabled students.

1

2

3

4

5

6

1. The Lloyd's Building, London
Modern ramp to a hi–tec building.
2. Museum of Science and
Industry, Manchester
Tactile cues and changes in
surface texture to identify the top
of the flight of steps.
3. The Museum of Scotland,
Chambers Street, Edinburgh
Unobtrusive location for a short
rise lift.
4. British Library, London
Carefully detailed internal ramp
located in an opened planned
atrium.
5. British Library, London
Guardrail and additional handrail
used for guidance and support.
6. Southwark Cathedral, London
Handrail projected and wreathed
at the commencement of a flight,
easy to grip for those with
manipulatory and hand
impairments. Steps with contrast
treads and risers.

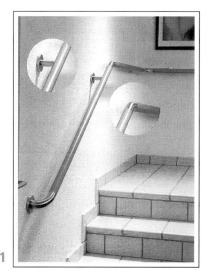

1. Handrail extended beyond the top and bottom of a flight and continues around half landings as a safety cue for those with visual impairments.
2. Princess Gate, London
Handrail projected to allow for easy identification of the commencement of the steps.
3. Walled Garden, Sunbury, Middlesex Peninsula sited toilet with oblique and lateral transfer space at the side of WC.
4. Automatic handwashing taps avoid the need to turn or twist taps.

4 Communication techniques for sensory or cognitively impaired audiences

However accessible the built environment may be, for the enjoyment of performing arts events it will be enhanced by having in place communication systems for patrons with sensory or cognitive impairments.

The functional purpose of an arts venue can only be achieved when the visitor, making the most sense of a performance or presentation, is able to participate, listen and enjoy performances or presentations which are fulfilling and inspirational.

Communication systems for visually impaired audiences

Vocaleyes

This is a nationwide audio description service providing access to the best in theatre and the arts.

Describers follow the performance and transmit the action that is taking place live on stage.

The event is described to the visitor by a discreet stethoscope-designed headset which can be adjusted in volume.

Before performances Vocaleyes issue tape recordings which give advanced information about a theatre, its access and facilities.

Vocaleyes also provide training for theatres to design and present their own audio described performances.

Audio description

This system is designed for people with visual impairments where a play, live on stage, can be described by an independent viewer.

Audio description aims to fill out the picture. It is the art of talking pictorially, making theatre a domain more easily enjoyed by those who cannot see. The set, costumes, facial expressions and action are described in a live commentary relayed on infra-red or radio through a headset. The description is live with the describer situated in a sound-proof box having a view of the stage, or in a room with a live video linkup.

It allows a set and the actions of the performers to be described when there is no speech. Trained audio describers research the script and attend rehearsals to assess what needs to be described in addition to the audible dialogue of the performers.

Audio introduction (some theatres only provide the 'Introductions')

Live or pre-recorded audio introductions use the same equipment as audio description to give a scripted synopsis of sets, costumes and characterisation before a performance starts or between acts.

Advance information

Recordings on tape or as Braille or large print versions of theatre programmes, cast lists and venue details can be offered, in addition to communication systems in resource centres and at pre-performance talks.

Touch tours

This allows visually impaired patrons who pre-book to have guided access to the stage before curtain up, meet members of the cast and touch props and costumes.

Hand-held audio guides assist exhibition visitors with visual impairment to form their own interpretation by providing carefully researched visual information on the works presented.

Communication systems for the visually impaired (libraries, archive and resource rooms)

The Kurzweil 1000

The Kurzweil system is an advanced reading tool for people who are blind or severely visually impaired.

The components are a personal computer used in conjunction with a flat bed scanner converting the printed word into synthetic speech.

Users can adjust reading speed, pitch and emphasis to suit specific references or needs. They can edit or create documents assisted by an audible dictionary or spell checker.

If a Braille file is opened the programme automatically performs a reverse Braille translation so that its contents can be read.

The system used in many libraries and resource centres was invented by Ray Kurzweil in 1976.

Cicero

Cicero is an alternative service that effectively takes a person's computer and scanner and turns them into a reading machine. Printed text documents are placed on the scanner and can then be translated into speech, Braille or simply held as a text document that can be adjusted, saved, edited and printed out. Cicero starts talking automatically as soon as the page scan is complete, and is fast, accurate and easy to use. Cicero allows one to view a document on screen in large print with a selection of fonts and high contrast colours. It uses 'Recognita's 32-bit OCR engine, and works with Microsoft Windows 95, 98, Me, NT 4.0, 2000 and XP. The only special equipment needed is a Windows soundcard and a twain compatible scanner.

Jaws (Job Access With Speech)

This provides speech output technology via Windows 95/98/ME/XP home or Windows NT/2000/XP professional operating system.

This system incorporates an integrated voice synthesiser to speak information from what appears on the computer screen.

Jaws installs an enhanced multilingual software.

Screen magnification system

Screen magnification allows text lines and words to be enhanced to larger print size. This is sometimes used where a person has some residual vision.

Task lighting

Task lighting to provide intense illumination of text or exhibits under study can increase the legibility and visibility of viewers with visual impairment.

Communication systems for hearing impaired audiences

Stagetext

Stagetext is a captioned performance system that allows people with hearing loss, who are not helped by sign language interpretation or by induction loop or infra-red systems.

This was developed by people with a hearing loss who are enthusiastic about making the performing arts accessible.

Captions are shown electronically in a discreet position in the theatre simultaneously with the words spoken or being sung, providing scripted or live text in any language so that patrons can fully understand the performance.

Lipspeakers

Lipspeakers are specially trained to work with deaf and hard of hearing people who prefer to communicate through lipreading and speech.

Lipspeakers repeat what is said without using their voices.

They produce the shape of words with the flow, rhythm and phrasing of speech.

A listener needs to be a practised lipreader to use this communication method.

Sign language interpreters

Sign language interpreters are professionally trained to work with people who are fluent and use British Sign Language (BSL). Sign Supported English (SSE) communicates less information to people whose first language is BSL.

Interpreting is a mentally and physically demanding task.

The interpreter needs to be well illuminated and positioned in clear view of the sign readers. In performances the interpreter, facing the audience, may need to view a live video linkup.

Speech to Text Reporters (STT) – Palantype

Speech to text reporters key everything that is said into a computer so that it can be read.

The keyboard is designed to let the STT reporter type words phonetically, 'how they sound', rather than how they are spelt.

Fed into a computer with appropriate software, words can be converted back to English.

This method allows the reporter to keep up to speed with the spoken word.

The text can be relayed via a laptop, but for larger events the information can be projected onto a large screen.

STT reporters are referred to as Palantypists.

Induction loop system

For people with hearing aids the induction loop system acts as a highly effective block against background noise, so the loop assists users by reducing extraneous sound in halls and at booking and information counters.

It uses an electromagnetic wave radiation method of transmitting a signal to the listener who is using a hearing aid.

The induction loop system consists of a transmitter wire around the perimeter of a room, connected to an amplifier and microphone.

When the listener's hearing aid is switched to 'T' it is then tuned to receive speech from the loop microphone in use.

BS 6083 Part 4 standardises the output power of an induction loop system, so that however far the listener is from the person using a loop microphone, the listener can follow speech clearly and loudly.

For small rooms, as an alternative to the installation in a large meeting hall, the induction loop system can be portable. The portable unit can be a table or counter top transmitter, or be a pad placed under a cushion or at the back of a listener's chair.

An induction loop system does not provide confidentiality as it transmits through doors and walls. Other signals may be picked up from mobile phones or other electrical equipment or circuits, so fitted systems may lose clarity if not tested by panels of users and refitted at regular intervals.

Infra-red system

For high quality reproduction of speech and stage sound to those who have a hearing impairment, an infra-red system can be installed in larger areas and foyers.

The signals are transmitted from public address system microphones to infra-red system sound radiators, mounted near ceilings.

A hearing receiver is tuned into the transmission frequency of the system which transfers the signal directly from the microphone. The sound radiator in a theatre foyer will play a recorded message so that listeners can try out their receiver before entering an auditorium or performance space.

This provides high quality reception unaffected by lighting or electrical interference.

In the UK there are two types of infra-red hearing receivers offered. The first is a headset fitted onto the ears. The second, a neckloop receiver, transfers sound into a listener's hearing aid when this is switched to 'T'.

Two channel infra-red systems allow some listeners in an audience to receive speech from stage microphones at the same time as others are listening to stage sound and live commentary from an audio describer.

Text phones

Text phones are used by people who are deaf or speech impaired and who cannot use standard telephones, or between people in the deaf community whose first language is BSL, which has its own grammar and idioms.

A text phone sends typed conversation along a telephone line to a text phone at the other end of the line.

You can use a telephone to communicate with other text phone users by typing what you want to say.

Words appear on the screen of the telephone being used.

If a text phone user wants to call someone who has an ordinary voice telephone the National Relay Service run by the RNID on BT relays conversations between people who use text phones and people who use voice phones.

The Type Talk Team consists of specially trained operators.

You call the operator with your text phone and they contact the person you want to speak to. The operator passes on your message and types back their reply in complete confidence.

Audio described and signed television

Communication systems in auditoriums to assist people with visual or hearing impairments are often the by-products of new technology developments.

Audio description is becoming an area of communication not only used in 'live' theatre performances but is being developed for use in television transmission and for adding on to sound tracks of feature films projected in some cinemas.

The BBC and ITV are using Auditel for selected programmes for a trial period as part of audience research in association with the RNIB.

Picture-in-picture sign language interpretation should be planned prior to recording and editing material into video or broadcast programmes and presentations.

Intellectual assistance

Communication with people, not only for those with sensory impairments, but for those with cognitive limitations, needs understanding.

Cognition is the process by which knowledge is acquired.

In that process there are people with learning difficulties where perception, intuition, learning and reasoning are mental processes which are not so easily acquired.

Alternative solutions in which the management of the built environment is engaged, can be assisted by an interpreting facility.

Escorts and interpreters for people with learning difficulties is an important aid when offering equal opportunities to take part in an experience or an event in arts premises.

5 The International Symbol of Access (ISA)

Introduction

Rehabilitation International (RI) is a federation of 145 organisations in 82 countries conducting programmes to assist people with disabilities and all who work for prevention, rehabilitation and integration.

The idea of a Symbol of Access was accepted for international recommendation by the Assembly of RI at the 11th World Congress held in Dublin in September 1969. The design of Miss Susan Koefoed, Denmark, was proposed and adopted after six symbols had been judged by an independent and international jury. It became known as the Symbol of Access.

RI adopted resolutions for the use of the symbol but it has been found that the implementation and the use of the ISA varied considerably and the criteria for applying the symbol were inconsistent.

ICTA (International Commission on Technology and Accessibility) requested that an investigation be carried out to establish the current position which was entrusted to Johann Kaiser, Austria, and Wycliffe Noble, United Kingdom.

The report by them was presented at the ICTA Seminar of the 16th World Congress of Rehabilitation International in Tokyo (1988).

This led to the recommendation that a document on guidance should be prepared for the use of the ISA, bearing in mind the varying circumstances that exist in different countries.

Guidance on the use of ISA

1. It shall be the aim of every country to strive to achieve a built environment and provide facilities, which can be used by people with disabilities.
2. The planning guidelines for using the ISA are those set out in the 'Guidelines for Improving Access for Disabled People', ICTA – RADAR 1983.
3. In some countries this will require a programme of phased development in order to reach the ultimate level of provision as outlined in 1 and 2.
4. To achieve this and in these circumstances, the minimum level of provision in building design in a planned environment shall be:
    - a barrier-free approach to the building;
    - an accessible entrance;
    - accessible and usable facilities;
    - accessible and usable toilets.
5. This minimum level shall not be considered as the ultimate level and at all times the 15 clauses in the 'Guidelines for Improving Access for Disabled People' shall be the aim. This is to ensure a consistent provision that will be understood when the ISA is applied to a building.

Location

6. The ISA is an internationally recognisable primary information symbol and shall be displayed at the key points of first use.
7. The ISA shall be awarded to a building and can be displayed at its principal entrance, after the appropriate local organisation of disabled people shall have had an opportunity to inspect the building on the basis of the

ICTA criteria/guidelines and made recommendations to its local or national organisation.

8. The ISA may be displayed within a building at the entrance of a usable facility, e.g. toilet, lift, etc.

9. The ISA may be used on public transportation systems where the accessible facilities are usable.

Design

10. The copyright design for style, shape and proportion, approved by RI, shall be adopted at all times, and there should be no deviation from the International Standard ISO 7000.
    (The colours used for the ISA shall always be in sharp contrast and its background shall be produced in either black or dark blue with the symbol in white.)

11. The ISA may be used in conjunction with, and adjacent to, other internationally recognised traffic and pedestrian directional signs, but the ISA itself shall not incorporate in its design any other feature which would confuse the information being conveyed.

12. The use of the ISA may be incorporated as a logo by organisations, companies and publishers representing the views of people with disabilities, in brochures, documents and publications.

Other symbols

13. Other symbols particularly applicable to the sensory impaired are not excluded from use in a building where the ISA is displayed, if they positively provide additional guidance.

International Commission on Technology and Accessibility (ICTA)

The International Commission on Technology and Accessibility (ICTA) is a Standing Commission of RI.

The members of ICTA are in principle nominated by the (affiliate) member organisations of RI.

The ICTA Information Centre provides support to the ICTA Commission in its tasks.

Following social and technological changes, ICTA adopted its present name in 1989, in order to express the general influence of technology and accessibility for people with a disability on integration in society. The global plan of action, which was accepted by the Commission for the next period of work, will deal with:

- the physical accessibility of buildings and technological infrastructure;
- the access to data on products and technology and its use by disabled people;
- the access to services in society, which should become freely accessible to everybody;
- the exchange of experiences of the ICTA members.

Correspondence address

Rehabilitation International
25 East 21st Street
NEW YORK
New York 10010
USA

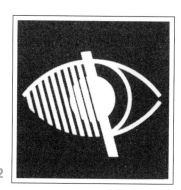

1. The International Symbol of Access.
2. The International Symbol for the
Visually Impaired.
3. The International Symbol for Guide
Dogs for the Blind.
4. The International Symbol for the
Hearing Impaired.

6 Legislation and standards

During the course of preparation of the book the legislative and advisory framework has changed, starting with the publication of the Disability Discrimination Act 1995, supplemented by the Disability Rights Commission Code of Practice – 'Rights of Access to Goods, Facilities, Services and Premises', 2002 Edition.

BS 8300 – New Part M Building Regulations

In October 2001 a new British Standard 8300: 2001 – 'Design of buildings and their approaches to meet the needs of disabled people – code of practice' was published. This is based on validated research evidence and in the future will form the basis of good practice recommendation, extending the previous limited scope of the earlier document BS 5810, which is now withdrawn. The revision to Building Regulations in the existent Approved Document Part M 1999 Edition will take this evidence into account.

The access provision currently being drafted is intended to complement the broad principles of the Disability Discrimination Act.

The principle of conforming to current regulations will have been followed by designers and incorporated in the buildings selected, so for each element of a building illustrated there will be no reference point to a regulation or particular standard.

The 'Provisions' of Approved Document M 'Access and Facilities for Disabled People' (1999 Edition) are not mandatory but provide guidance on one way of meeting the Requirements of the Regulation; its status is defined as follows:

> The Approved Documents are intended to provide guidance for some of the more common building situations. However, there may well be alternative ways of achieving compliance with the requirements.

Thus there is no obligation to adopt any particular solution contained in the present Approved Document if the relevant requirements are met in some other way.

The revised Approved Document M is expected to be published in 2004.

Provision of access for disabled people

The principal enactments

The Building Act 1984 (BA) which enables building regulations to be made to impose certain requirements on the built environment having regard to the use to which buildings are put.

For details see Briefing Note I (DSG-P1)

Sponsoring department – the Office of the Deputy Prime Minister (ODPM) advised by the Building Regulations Advisory Committee (BRAC)

The Disability Discrimination Act 1995 (DDA) which imposes certain duties on the providers of services to have regard to the needs of disabled people. It is supported by the Disability Rights Commission Act 1999 which created the Disability Rights Commission as an independent body to advise Government on the working of the DDA and to help to secure civil rights for disabled people.

For details see Briefing Note II (DSG-P2)

Sponsoring department – the Department for Work and Pensions advised by the Disability Rights Commission.

The Transport Act 1985 (TA) which created the Disabled Persons Transport Advisory Committee to advise the Secretary of State on matters which he refers to it and to advise him on matters which it thinks appropriate.

For details see Briefing Note III (DSG-P5)

Sponsoring department – the Department for Transport advised by the Disabled Persons Transport Advisory Committee (DPTAC).

Legislation for Scotland and Northern Ireland

Technical standards for compliance with the Building Standards (Scotland) Regulations. Part T: Access and facilities for disabled people. Edinburgh: The Stationery Office.

Building Regulations (Northern Ireland). Technical Booklet R: Access and facilities for disabled people. Belfast: The Stationery Office.

Appendix 1   The Disability Discrimination Act 1995

A Bridge to inclusion: The Disability Discrimination Act (DDA) 1995: this includes new requirements to make goods, facilities, services and premises more accessible to disabled people from 2004.

Code of Practice

On 1st October 2004 the final stage of Part III of the DDA – goods, facilities and services provisions – comes into operation. The new duties will apply to businesses and other providers of services to the public where physical features make access to their services impossible or unreasonably difficult for disabled people. The duties are a further step to ensuring that disabled people have access to services that others take for granted. It is important that service providers prepare for these new duties.

The Statutory Code of Practice provides detailed advice and is available as:

English print: ISBN 0 117028606
Welsh print: ISBN 0 117029270
Audio text: ISBN 0 117029297
Braille text: ISBN 0 117029289
Disk format: ISBN 0 117029300
From The Stationery Office (TSO)

Tel: 0870 600 5522
Fax: 0870 600 5533

or at a city TSO in London, Birmingham, Bristol, Manchester, Belfast, Cardiff and Edinburgh.
or order from a local bookshop
or online www.clicktso.com
or www.thestationeryoffice.com

Under the DDA it is unlawful to refuse to serve someone on the grounds of their disability or to charge disabled people more for a service.

From October 2004 all services and information will have to be accessible to disabled people. This may involve making guidelines and information leaflets available in large print or on tape, or installing a textphone to allow hearing impaired people to contact the provider. The law appears to cover services rather than buildings, so that, for example, owners of some offices can comply with the Act even if it is not possible to make the office fully accessible, provided that disabled people are not given a lower level of service. For example, if an owner normally requires applicants to come into the office for an interview, arrangements could be made to visit a disabled person at home or at another accessible place.

Discrimination

However, as it will be unlawful to discriminate against disabled people in the provision of goods, facilities and services, it is crucial for owners and managers of arts and heritage venues open to the public to examine access to their premises. Where a physical feature, including one related to the design or construction of the building or the approach or access to it, makes it impossible or unreasonably difficult for disabled people to make use of a particular service, the service provider has a duty to take such steps as are reasonable, in all the circumstances of the situation, to

- Remove the feature.
- Alter it so it no longer creates the difficulty.
- Provide a reasonable means of avoiding the feature.
- Provide a reasonable alternative way of making the building, or its service available to disabled people.

Training is an important feature for staff of public venues and businesses, and owners and managers should

- Examine the extent of training opportunities that may exist for improving attitudes towards disabled people, and the needs of their staff.
- Consider how these opportunities could improve the integration of and equality of opportunity.
- Assess the success or otherwise of the company in providing training and special facilities for face to face contact.

Effective access to buildings and relevant training is often not simple, and it is wise to seek the advice of an experienced individual or company skilled in the provision of access audits and advice and of training. The ADAPT Trust can assist in this way.

What it means for you

In addition to the Code, the Disability Rights Commission (DRC) has issued two booklets with this title that summarise the duties. One is for service providers; the other details the rights of disabled people. The DRC also has a number of advisory leaflets as case studies for particular small businesses.

The DRC Helpline is by voice, text, fax, post or email at any time between 08:00 and 20:00 Monday to Friday.

Telephone: 08457 622633
Textphone: 08457 622644
Fax: 08457 778878
Email: enquiry@drc-gb.org

Website:	www.drc-gb.org
Post:	DRC Helpline, Freepost, MID 02164 Stratford upon Avon CV37 9BR

Appendix 2   The ADAPT Trust

In 1977, when Geoffrey Lord was appointed Secretary and Treasurer to the Carnegie UK Trust, the arts policies were not a priority for the Trustees. A few individual grants were assisting artists to teach and engage disabled people in the arts, but these were isolated experiments and there was no link between the individuals or ideas.

Following two seminars[1] Geoffrey Lord established, with Trust support, the UK 'Inquiry into Arts and Disabled People', chaired by Sir Richard (now Lord) Attenborough. Sir Richard was then filming *Ghandi*, in India and it was not for him an easy decision that he should commit a substantial amount of time to chair a three-year inquiry into a topic that was to assess activities and would likely lead to all sorts of unknown ramifications from the desires of disabled or older people. There were many obstacles.

During the inquiry there was not one arts or heritage venue that was effectively accessible: the Brighton Festival was the only venue with reasonable access for wheelchair users. Indeed it proved impossible to find a venue in any region

[1] *The Arts and Disabilities* (1981) is a summary of the two seminars, and describes the background to several artistic services with disabled people and the conclusions from the seminars for future action. It is available for cost of postage from the Carnegie UK Trust, Comely Park House, Dunfermline, KY12 7EJ.
ISBN 0 904265 62

that provided effective access for a series of 12 regional conferences throughout the UK involving disabled people.

At the time the needs of wheelchair users were paramount, but the needs of ambulant disabled, deaf, blind and older people and those with other impairments, many disabled, had then – and now – to be covered. These seminars were a learning experience for all involved – staff, committee, participants and government – in providing temporary access and avoiding embarrassment when involving and assisting disabled people.

When the inquiry reported in 1985[2] it was clear that a large amount of work had to be undertaken to ensure that the recommendations were acted upon and that access to premises was a key factor in ensuring that all disabled people and older people had an equal opportunity to gain access to arts and heritage venues. The Carnegie Trustees agreed to fund the successor 'Carnegie Council' – chaired by the late Sir Kenneth Robinson – for two years to ensure progress.[3]

Access was the dominant challenge repeated in letters from disabled and older people throughout the UK; stories of frustration and annoyance at the lack of access and of additional obstacles by the attitude of staff at venues were embarrassing.

During the inquiry Simon Goodenough, a writer and publisher, had interviewed over 100 artists, several physically disabled,

[2] *Arts and Disabled People* (The Attenborough Report) (1985) includes the main recommendations of the Committee of Inquiry, but is now out of print. Published for the Carnegie UK Trust by Bedford Square Press, London.
ISBN 0 7199 1145 1

[3] *After Attenborough* (The Carnegie Council Review) (1988) reports on follow-up action and how various projects, including 'Arts for Health' in Manchester were established. Published for the Carnegie UK Trust by Bedford Square Press, London.
ISBN 0 7199 1234 2

and the Carnegie Trustees agreed to publish 50 of the most significant interviews.[4]

The Carnegie Trustees backed Lord's judgement that a new Trust was required to concentrate on access, and with a substantial grant the ADAPT Trust was registered as a charity in 1989 after preliminary work.

This included valuable support from the then Government Office of Arts and Libraries where the supportive Minister for the Arts, Sir Richard (now Lord) Luce, matched the initial grant in partnership, thus building on a commitment for a civil servant to be a participatory member of the inquiries.

The title 'ADAPT' emerged after the initial meeting in London of the Founding Trustees to consider a Trust Deed. An initial £1 million was raised to provide pump-priming grants to arts and heritage venues that showed interest in disabled and older people as consumers. ADAPT has now raised and distributed over £3 million and encouraged adaptations valued at over £6 million from its grant schemes and other advisory and consultancy services to over 300 venues.[5]

Many owners believed then that the cost of access was out of proportion to the commercial return, and some still use this as

[4]*Artability.* Simon Goodenough (1989) Michael Russell Publishing Ltd, Wilton, Wilts.
ISBN 0 85955 159 8
[5]The ADAPT Trust, a Scottish charity, No. SCO 20814, operating in the United Kingdom issues a regular newsletter obtainable from its office at:

Wellpark, 120 Sydney Street
Glasgow G31 1JF.
Telephone: 0141 556 2233
Fax: 0141 556 7799
Email: adapt.trust@virgin.net

The Trust has a CD Rom 'Open Sesame – The Magic of Access: Designing Access for Disabled People' available in PC and Mac format from its office.

Its website is currently being reorganised: details from the office.

an excuse to do little, but this argument quickly proved false. Effective access does not come cheap or easy or without planning, but it is worthwhile and also cost-effective. Effective access provision is a gateway and gives freedom to those wishing to enjoy the arts and performances thus enriching the spirit.

Appendix 3 ADAPT Grants and Awards and Founding Trustees

Since commencement the Trust has raised funds and co-operated with funding agencies to provide grants to arts and heritage venues for the improvement of access.

The Trust has also been assisted by companies and individuals to provide awards, a main award comprising a grant and a framed certificate, and a Highly Commended award with a certificate for display, to those venues that had accomplished effective access. This is a summary of the grants and awards.

ADAPT grants

1990–2001
149 grants total £1 377 030

1995–1998
'Capital Access' to London venues (with London Arts Board):
32 grants total £149 779

1998–2000
'Railtrack' grants to museums:
83 grants total £193 344

1995–2002
'Sightline' grants (Guide Dogs for the Blind Association) continuing:
97 grants total £325 797.

ADAPT awards

1992–1996
17 awards total £75 000
18 Highly Commended

1998–2001
18 awards total £45 000
16 Highly Commended

Founding Trustees

30 November 1992
Emma Nicholson MP (Chairman)
Robert F Donaldson
Trevan Hingston
Rachel Hurst
Geoffrey Lord OBE (Hon. Director)
The Lord Murray of Epping Forest
C Wycliffe Noble OBE
Henry Wrong CBE

Trustees and Office Bearers 2003

Michael Cassidy (Chairman)
The Hon. Mrs Elizabeth Fairbairn
Gary Flather OBE
John C Griffiths
Alison Heath MBE
Trevan Hingston
Robin Hyman
Maurice Paterson
Rita Tushingham
(Dr Gill Burrington OBE retired as Chairman in November 2002)

Bibliography

Recent relevant publications

Statutory references

The Building Regulations 1991: Access and facilities for disabled people. Approved Document M. 1999 edition
ISBN 0 11 753469 2
The Stationery Office
London
and outlets
General enquiries: 0870 600 5522
Fax: 0870 600 5533
Website: www.clicktso.co.uk

Also Building Control: list of all Building Regulations
Website: www.buildingcontrol.org

Building Regulations (Northern Ireland) 2000
ISBN 0 337 01096 X
The Stationery Office
Belfast
Website: www.dfpmi.com

Technical Standards for Compliance with the Building Standards (Scotland) Regulations. 1990, as amended
ISBN 0 11 497294 X (Bound)
0 11 497295 8 (Looseleaf)
The Stationery Office
Edinburgh

The Scottish Executive website includes all technical standards:
www.scotland.gov.uk/developments/bc

Code of Practice for the Design of Buildings and their Approaches to Meet the Needs of Disabled People
BS 8300-2. British Standards Institution (BSI) 2001
and
Fire Precautions in the Design, Construction and Use of Buildings – Code of Practice for Means of Escape for Disabled People. BS 5588: Part 8: 1988. BSI
British Standards Institution
389 Chiswick High Road
London W4 4AL
Tel: 0208 996 9000

Also note: E&W regulations and Approved Documents
Website: www.safety.odpm.gov.uk/bregs/brads.htm
Note that the Technical Standards and the Approved Documents may be downloaded free from the Government websites.

Guidance on the Use of Tactile Paving Surfaces.
Department of the Environment, Transport and The Regions, London, and The Scottish Office, Edinburgh. 1998
Product Code 99Mu0024
From: DETR Mobility Unit
Zone 1/11
76 Marsham Street
London SW1P 4DR
Tel: 0207 8906100.
Website:
www.mobilityunit.detr.gov.uk/guide/tactile/index.htm

Guide to Safety at Sports Grounds. 1997
The Stationery Office
ISBN 0 11 300095 2

Inclusive Mobility: a guide to best practice on access to pedestrian and transport infrastructure, by Philip R Oxley, Cranfield Centre for Logistics and Transportation
From: Department for Transport, Disability Policy Branch, Mobility and Inclusion Unit, Zone 1/18, Great Minster House, 76 Marsham Street, London SW1P 4DR
Tel: 020 7944 6100
Fax: 020 7944 6102
Email: miu@dft.gov.uk
Website: www.mobility-unit.dft.gov.uk

Disability Discrimination Act 1995
Various Codes of Practice, namely:
Rights of Access, Goods, Facilities, Service and Premises.
DfEE
ISBN numbers are:
English print 0117028606
Welsh print 0117029270
Audio 0117029297
Braille 0117029289
Disk 0117029300

Elimination of Discrimination in the Field of Employment Against Disabled Persons or Persons who have had a Disability. DfEE
and
Duties of Trade Organisations to their Disabled Members and Applicants. DfEE
NB: The only available source for these publications is: The Stationery Office, London and its other outlets in Belfast, Birmingham, Bristol, Manchester, Cardiff and Edinburgh.
Enquiries: 0870 600 5522. Fax: 0870 600 5533, or online: www.clicktso.co.uk

Access to the Built Heritage – technical advice note 7.
1996
Historic Scotland, Edinburgh
ISBN 1 900168 23 5

Housing for Varying Needs, a design guide, Part 1 – houses and flats. Scottish Homes
ISBN 0 11 495884X
The Stationery Office

Overcoming the Barriers: providing physical access to historic buildings
CADW – Welsh Historic Monuments. 2002
ISBN 1 85760 104 1

Other publications

Access Audits: a guide and checklists for appraising the accessibility of public buildings
Andrew Lacey. 1999
ISBN 0 903976 30 7
and
Access to ATMs: UK design guidelines
Robert Feeney. 2002
ISBN 0 903976 33 1
and
Designing for Accessibility: an essential guide for public buildings
Andrew Lacey. 1999
ISBN 0 903976 31 5

Other booklets (see below under 'Information') from:

Centre for Accessible Environments
Nutmeg House
60 Gainsford Street
London SE1 2NY
Tel: 0207 357 8182
Website: www.cae.org.uk

Access in Mind – towards the inclusive museum
Ann Rayner, The Intellectual Access Trust. 1998
National Museum of Scotland
Edinburgh
ISBN 1 901663 18 3

Access to Arts Buildings
Ian Appleton. 1995
Scottish Arts Council
Edinburgh
ISBN 185 11 9 0783

Access to the Historic Environment
Lisa Foster. 1997
Donhead Publishing, Shaftesbury
ISBN 1 873394 18 7

Barrier-free Design: a manual for building designers and managers
James Holmes-Siedle. 1996
Butterworth Architecture
ISBN 0 7506 1636 9

Buildings for All to Use: good practice guidance for improving existing public buildings for people with disabilities
Sylvester Bone. 1996
Construction Industry Research and Information Association (CIRIA)
ISBN 0 860177 448 4

Building Sight: a handbook of building and interior design solutions to include the needs of visually impaired people
Peter Barker, Jon Barrick and Rod Wilson. 1995
Royal National Institute for the Blind (RNIB)
ISBN 1 85878 057 8 (hardback)
ISBN 1 85878 074 8 (paperback)

Designing Exhibitions to Include People with Disabilities
Gail Nolan. 1997
National Museum of Scotland
Edinburgh
ISBN 1 901663 00 0

Disability: making buildings accessible – Special Report 2002
(Essential guidance on law, regulations, policy and practice)
Keith Bright, Research Group for Inclusive Environments
The University of Reading
ISBN 1 900648 14 8

Disability Resource Directory for Museums, and Supplement. 1997
Resource for Museums and Galleries Commission
London

European Concept for Access
Maryan van Zvylen –
Secretary General, Central Co-ordinating Commission for the Promotion of Accessibility (CCPT)
The Netherlands. 1995
and
Handicap, Architecture and Design
Poul Ostergaard, Aarhus School of Architecture. 1997
Christian Ejlers Publishers, Postbox 2228. DK 1018 KBH.K.
Denmark. (CD Rom with 1000 video clips)
Distribution in UK:
European Institute for Design and Disability, Special Needs Research Unit, University of Northumbria, Coach Lane Campus, Newcastle upon Tyne, NE7 7TW
ISBN 877 77241 191 0

In Through the Front Door (disabled people and the visual arts – examples of good practice)
Jane Earnscliffe, Arts Council of England
ISBN 0 72877 0649 0

Increasing Access to the Wider Countryside for Disabled People
FieldfareTrust Sheffield and Countryside Agency.
Cheltenham. 2001
and
Paths without Prejudice
CAX 57. C.A. Cheltenham. 2001
and
Sense and Accessibility. CAX26. C.A. Cheltenham. 2000
Enquiries to the Countryside Agency Library. Cheltenham
Tel: 01242 521381

Minimum Standards for Access for New and Reconstructed Buildings
Tom Lister. 1995
Heriot-Watt University, Edinburgh and Central Regional
Council

Open for Business: a best practice guide on access
David Bonnett and Patrick Tolfree. Undated
EFD

Perspectives on Access to Museums and Galleries in Historic Buildings
Lisa Foster and Alison Coles. 1996
The Museums and Galleries Commission
16 Queen Anne's Gate
London SW1H 9AA
(free with A4 SAE)
ISBN 0 948630 49 3

Policy into Practice – Disability
Ruth Bailey
Independent Theatre Council. 2001
Tel: 0207 403 1727
ISBN 1 871180 09 0

The Big Foot – museums and children with learning difficulties
Anne Pearson and Chitra Aloysius
British Museum Press
ISBN 0 7141 1744 77

The Disability Discrimination Act: inclusion – a workbook for building owners, facilities managers and architects
John H Penton. 1999
RIBA Publications

101 Ways to Implement the DDA
Eleanor Wilson
Institute of Leisure and Amenity Management. 2001
ISBN 1 873903 91 X

Through the Roof
Paul Dicken
Roof Breaker Guides
Edition 4 – 2002

Widening the Eye of the Needle: access to church buildings for people with disabilities
John Penton. 2001
Church House Publishing
ISBN 0 7151 7587 4

Publications produced by the Carnegie UK Trust

The Arts and Disabilities – a creative response to social handicap
Geoffrey Lord. 1981
MacDonald Publishers Edinburgh
ISBN 0 904265 62 5

Arts and Disabled People
(The Attenborough Report) 1985 includes the main recommendations of the Committee of Inquiry, but is now out of print. Published for the Carnegie UK Trust by Bedford Square Press, London
ISBN 0 7199 1145 1

After Attenborough
(The Carnegie Council Review) 1988 reports on follow-up
action and how various projects, including 'Arts for Health'
in Manchester were established. Published for the Carnegie
UK Trust by Bedford Square Press, London
ISBN 0 7199 1234 2

Enquiries for these publications may be made to the
Carnegie UK Trust office
Tel: 01383 721345

Publication produced by the ADAPT Trust

*Open Sesame – the magic of access, designing access for
disabled people.* 1999
CDRom and Pocket Guide
ISBN 0 9529030 2 4
Email: adapt.trust@virgin.net
Tel: 0141 556 2233
Fax: 0141 556 7799

Information

Several agencies have a website for information on access,
but please note that the Internet has 282 000 entries under
the title 'Access to buildings' so that access to particular
information requires a specific search reference, such as
'Building Control Regulations', perhaps through Google, to
achieve success.

Information is available, normally free of charge for a charity
(suggest enclosing a large SAE), at these contacts:

Aware Photographic Arts
4 Sefton Grove
Lark Lane
Liverpool L17 8XB
Tel: 0151 727 7421. *Mobile Photographic Unit for Access*

Building Control: list of all Building Regulations
Websites: www.buildingcontrol.orgwww.dfpmi.com
(for Northern Ireland)
www.scotland.gov.uk/developments/bc
(for Scotland)

Centre for Accessible Environments
Nutmeg House
60 Gainsford Street
London SE1 2NY
Tel: 020 7357 8182
Publications 2002 including:
Reading and Using Plans £10.
Keeping Up with the Past: making historic buildings
accessible to everyone Video £14.10
Automatic Door Controls £2.50
Internal Floor Finishes £2.50

Department of the Environment
Mobility Unit
Transport and the Regions
Zone 1/11
Great Minster House
76 Marsham Street
London SW1P 4DR
Tel: 0207 890 6100
Guidance on the Use of Tactile Paving Surfaces

Disability Advice Centre
Website: DAC@consignia.com
Disability Rights Commission
Information & Legislation
Freepost MID 02164
Stratford upon Avon CV37 9BR
Helpline: 08457 622633
Textphone: 08457 622644
Website: www.drc-gb.org/drc/information
Includes response to CADW consultation and various
Codes of Practice for downloading free

GDBA: Guide Dogs for the Blind Association
Hillfields
Burghfield Common
Reading RG7 3YG
Tel: 0118 9838281
Website: www.guidedogs.org.uk
Guide Dog Owners Countdown to Top 10 Obstacles

Office of the Deputy Prime Minister
Website: www.odpm.gov.uk/news/0208/0060
'Government proposes tough new rules to open buildings to all'

Royal Association of Disability and Rehabilitation
12 City Forum
250 City Road
London EC1V 8AF
Tel: 0207 250 3222
Access Data Sheet
and
Rehabilitation International – guidance on the use of the International Symbol of Access
and
Rehabilitation International – Commission on Technology and Accessibility: directives pour une meilleure accessibilité de l'environnement aux personnes handicapées
Author: C Wycliffe Noble

National Disability Arts Forum
MEA House
Ellison Place
Newcastle upon Tyne NE1 8XS
Tel: 0191 261 1628
Website: www.ndaf.org.uk
Disability Arts Forums are local groups of disabled people with a particular interest in the arts, to provide advice and information on accessibility

Royal National Institute for the Blind
Joint Mobility Unit Technical Bulletins
105 Judd Street
London WC1H 9NE
Tel: 020 7388 1266
Fax: 020 7388 2034

See it Right Pack. 2001

Pedestrian Environment, Sign Design, Lighting, Colour-tone Contrasting, etc.
and
Design Guide to the Use of Colour and Contrast to Improve the Built Environment for Visually Impaired People (with ICI Dulux)
and
Keeping Step – scientific and technological research for visually impaired people.
John Gill. 2001
RNIB Scientific Research Unit
Also
Sign Design Guide
Peter Barker and June Fraser
ISBN 185 878 4123
From: Sign Design Society
66 Derwent Road
Kinsbourne Green
Harpenden
Herts AL5 3NX

Royal National Institute for Deaf People
19–23 Featherstone Street
London EC1Y 8SL
Queries to information line:
Tel: 0808 808 0123
Textphone: 0808 808 9000
Fax: 020 7296 8199
Email: informationline@rnid.org.uk
Website: www.rnid.org.uk

Induction Loop and Infrared Systems – information for people managing public venues

Also information from:
RNID Sound Advantage,
1 Metro Centre
Welbeck Way
Peterborough PE2 7UH
Tel: 01733 232607
Website: www.mid.org.uk
Lightweight Textphones and Portable Induction Loops etc

Traffic Director for London
College House
Great Peter Street
London SW1P 3LN
Tel: 0207 233 0061
Advice on the design of side-road entry treatments on priority (red) routes in London

Voluntary Arts Network
PO Box 200
Cardiff CF5 1YH
Tel: 0292 039 5395
VAN Briefings: eg, Creating Clear Print – reaching the blind and partially sighted
A useful series of advisory leaflets about access

A new website especially for disabled people is:
www.wheelchairaccess.fsnet.co.uk
This contains information, supplied by venues, on access facilities, covering a range of venues and services primarily in cities in the UK

Welsh Accessibility Initiative (WAI)
Web content accessibility
www.w3.org/wai

Commercial contacts for special products

Cityspace: Retec
17–29 West Greenhill Place
Glasgow G3 8LL
Tel: 0141 248 4333
Accessible counters for all your customers

Movement Management Ltd
123 Abbey Lane
Leicester LE4 5QX
Tel: 0116 225 2100
Platform lifts etc.

Paraid, Paraid House
Weston Lane
Birmingham B11 3RS
Tel: 0121 7066744
EVAC +Chair – The World's First Stairway Evacuation

Portaramp – Roman House
Roman Way
Fison Way Industrial Estate
Thetford Norfolk IP24 1HT
Tel: 01842 750186
Portable and Module Ramps

Rediweld Rubber and Plastics Ltd
6/8 Newman Lane
Alton
Hampshire GU34 2QR
Tel: 01420 543007
Takpave – a range of rubber tiles providing tactile surfaces for the guidance of visually impaired people both indoors and outdoors

List of contacts for each venue

BFI London IMAX® Cinema, London

BFI London IMAX Cinema
1 Charlie Chaplin Walk
South Bank
Waterloo
LONDON SE1 8XR

Tel: 020 7960 3100
Duty Manager: 020 7960 3180
www.bfi.org.uk/imax

Brixworth Library, Northampton

I J Clarke – Principal Librarian West
Tel: 01327 703130

Brixworth Library
Spratton Road
Brixworth
Northampton NN6 9DS

Tel: 01604 882153
Fax: 01604 882154
www.Northamptonshire.gov.uk

Edinburgh Castle

Barbara Smith – Castle Manager (Technical Enquiries)
Barbara Fraser – Press and Publicity Manager (General Enquiries)

Historic Scotland
Longmore House
Salisbury Place
EDINBURGH
EH9 1SH

Tel: 0131 668 8600
Fax: 0131 668 8741
www.historic-scotland.gov.uk

Grosvenor Museum, Chester

Charles Quinn – Visitor Services Officer
Tel: 01244 402010

Grosvenor Museum
27 Grosvenor Street
CHESTER
CH1 2DD

Tel.No: 01244 402008
Fax No: 01244 347587
www.chestercc.gov.uk/heritage/museum/home

Museum of Science and Industry, Manchester

R L Scott – Acting Director

The Museum of Science and Industry in Manchester
Liverpool Road
Castlefield
MANCHESTER
M3 4FP

Tel: 0161 832 2244
Fax: 0161 606 0104
www.msim.org.uk

The Museum of Worcester Porcelain, Worcester

Amanda Savidge – Museum Manager

The Museum of Worcester Porcelain
Severn Street
WORCESTER
WR1 2NE

Tel: 01905 746000
Fax: 01905 617807
www.worcesterporcelainmuseum.org

National Railway Museum, York

Andrew Scott – Head of Museum
National Railway Museum
Leeman Road
YORK
YO26 4XJ

Tel: 01904 621261
Fax: 01904 611112
www.nrm.org.uk

Papworth Everard Library, Cambridgeshire

Mrs Leonore Charlton – Development and Marketing
Manager
Tel: 01480 375193

Papworth Everard Library
Pendrill Court
Papworth Everard

CAMBRIDGESHIRE
CB3 8UY

Tel.: 01480 830940
Fax: 01480 830940
www.cambridgeshire.gov.uk/library

RADA (Royal Academy of Dramatic Art), London

Royal Academy of Dramatic Art
62–64 Gower Street
LONDON
WC1E 6ED

Tel: 0207 636 7076
Fax: 0207 323 3865
www.rada.org.uk

Royal Albert Hall, London

Ian Blackburn – Former Director of Building Development

Royal Albert Hall
Kensington Gore
LONDON
SW7 2AP

Tel: 020 7589 3203
Fax: 020 7823 9095
www.royalalberthall.com

Royal Shakespeare Company, Stratford upon Avon

Pat Collcutt – Access Officer
Mobile: 07714 243868

Royal Shakespeare Theatre
Waterside

STRATFORD UPON AVON
Warwickshire
CV37 6BB

Tel: 01789 412660
Fax: 01789 294810
www.rsc.org.uk

Somerset House, London

Donne Robertson – Director of Events and Access

Somerset House Trust
Somerset House
Strand
LONDON
WC2R 1LA

Tel: 020 7836 8686
Fax: 020 7836 7613
www.somerset-house.org.uk

Palace of Westminster, London

Parliamentary Works Directorate

House of Commons
Accommodation and Works Committee
LONDON
SW1A 0AA

Royal National Theatre, London

Ros Hayes – Senior House Manager

South Bank
LONDON
SE1 9PX

Tel: 020 7452 3333
www.nationaltheatre.org.uk

National Portrait Gallery, London

Lucy Ribeiro – Access Officer

St Martin's Place
LONDON
WC2H 0HE

Tel: 020 7306 0055
www.npg.org.uk

Index

Page numbers in **bold** type indicate illustrations.
Colour plates are indicated in **bold** type by the letters '**CP**' with a relevant number.